Mathematics Olympiad

Highly useful for all school students participating
in Various Olympiads & Competitions

Series Editor Keshav Mohan
Author Priya Mittal

Class 4

arihant

ARIHANT PRAKASHAN, MEERUT

ARIHANT PRAKASHAN, MEERUT
All Rights Reserved

卐 **Administrative & Production Offices**

Corporate Office 'Ramchhaya' 4577/15, Agarwal Road, Darya Ganj New Delhi -110002
Tele: 011- 47630600, 43518550; Fax: 011- 23280316

Head Office Kalindi, TP Nagar, Meerut (UP) - 250002
Tele: 0121-2401479, 2512970, 4004199; Fax: 0121-2401648

All disputes subject to Meerut (UP) jurisdiction only.

卐 **Sales & Support Offices**

Agra, Ahmedabad, Bengaluru, Bhubaneswar, Bareilly, Chennai, Delhi, Guwahati, Haldwani, Hyderabad, Jaipur, Jalandhar, Jhansi, Kolkata, Kota, Lucknow, Meerut, Nagpur & Pune

卐 **ISBN**   978-93-5251-207-2

卐 **Price**   ₹65

Typeset by Arihant DTP Unit at Meerut
Printed & Bound by Arihant Publications (I) Ltd. (Press Unit)

Production Team

Publishing Manager	Mahendra Singh Rawat	Page Layouting	Vijay Saini
Project Head	Mona Yadav	DTP Operator	Deepak Kumar
Project Coordinator	Himanshu Verma	Cover Designer	Syed Darin Zaidi
Proof Reader	Knishu Sharma	Inner Designer	Deepak Kumar

For further information about the products from Arihant
log on to www.arihantbooks.com or email to info@arihantbooks.com

Preface

Mathematics Olympiad Series for Class 2nd-10th is a series of books which will challenge the young inquisitive minds by the non-routine and exciting mathematical problems.

The main purpose of this series is to make the students ready for competitive exams. The school/board exams are of qualifying nature but not competitive, they do not help the students to prepare for competitive exams, which mainly have objective questions.

- **Need of Olympiad Series**
  This series will fill this gap between the school/board and competitive exams as this series have all questions in Objective format. This series helps students who are willing to sharpen their problem solving skills. Unlike typical assessment books, which emphasis on drilling practice, the focus of this series is on practicing problem solving techniques.

- **Development of Logical Approach**
  The thought provoking questions given in this series will help students to attain a deeper understanding of the concepts and through which students will be able to impart Reasoning/Logical/Analytical skills in them.

- **Complement Your School Studies**
  This series complements the additional preparation needs of students for regular school/board exams. Along with, it will also address all the requirements of the students who are approaching National/State level Olympiads.

I shall welcome criticism from the students, teachers, educators and parents. I shall also like to hear from all of you about errors and deficiencies, which may have remained in this edition and the suggestions for the next edition.

Editor

Contents

Knowing Our Numbers

Numbers are mathematical objects by which we express date time, position, quantity, etc. Numbers are written by using digits such as 0, 1, 2, 3, ...

Indian place value system chart

Crore	Ten lakh	Lakh	Ten thousand	Thousand	Hundred	Tens	Ones
1,00,00,000	10,00,000	1,00,000	10,000	1,000	100	10	1

International place value system chart

Million	Hundred thousand	Ten thousand	Thousand	Hundred	Tens	Ones
1,000,000	100,000	10,000	1,000	100	10	1

Face value   The face value of a digit is the digit itself.

e.g.   Face value of 9 in 1936 is 9 itself.

Place value   When we multiply face value of the digit with the value of its period, it will give its place value. e.g.   Place value of 6 in 65329 is 60000.

Rounding off to nearest ten   Numbers whose unit digits end in 5 or more should be rounded upto the next ten. The numbers whose unit digits end in less than 5 should be rounded to previous ten. e.g.   88 should be rounded off to 90 and 84 should be rounded off to 80.

Rounding off to nearest hundred   Numbers whose last two digits (at unit and tens place) are less than 50 should be rounded off to the previous hundred whereas the numbers that have the last two digits equal to 50 or more should be rounded off to the next hundred. e.g. 424 should be rounded off to 400 and 464 should be rounded off to 500.

Roman numerals   Roman numerals are based on the following symbols :

1	5	10	50	100	500	1000
I	V	X	L	C	D	M

e.g. VI = 6, IX = 9, XX = 20, XXIX = 29

Let's Practice

1. There are eighty six thousand four hundred seconds in a day. How else could this number be written?
   (a) 80064   (b) 80640
   (c) 86400   (d) 86404

2. Two persons were having an amount of ₹ 435900 and ₹ 455500, respectively. What is the place value of '4' in the total amount of both the persons?
   (a) 40   (b) 400   (c) 40000   (d) 400000

3. A teacher while teaching wrote some numbers as given below, in which all are same except one. The one which is different, will be
   (a) 100 ones   (b) 10 tens
   (c) 1 hundred   (d) 100 tens

4. The jar shows the rounded figure to nearest ten. How many balls could be there in the jar? 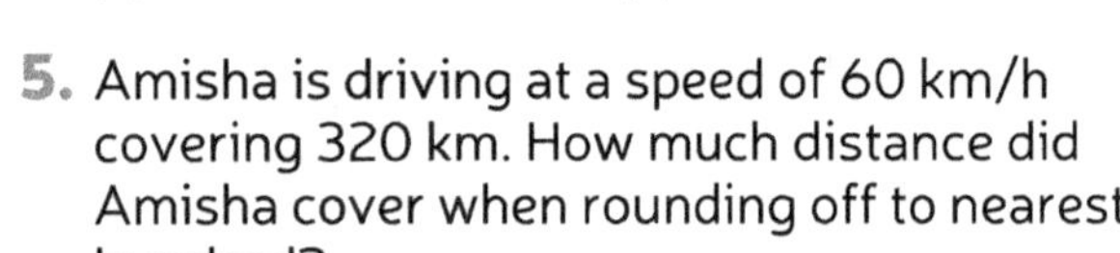
   (a) 295   (b) 260
   (c) 345   (d) 280

5. Amisha is driving at a speed of 60 km/h covering 320 km. How much distance did Amisha cover when rounding off to nearest hundred?
   (a) 300   (b) 350   (c) 330   (d) 325

6. 596280 = 500000 + ☐ + ☐ + ☐ + 80
   Which three numbers should be used to fill the boxes correctly?
   (a) 90000, 6000, 200   (b) 60000, 9000, 200
   (c) 9000, 60000, 200   (d) 9000, 6000, 20

7. Sonia reads some pages every month given in the table below. In which month, did she read the least number of pages?

Months	Number of pages
January	6916
February	6906
March	6876
April	6887

(a) January   (b) February
(c) March   (d) April

8. A book has 160 pages. How many page numbers contain the digit '0' ?
   (a) 20   (b) 25
   (c) 26   (d) 27

9. Which number out of the given choices should be inserted in the box, so that the given series is in ascending order?

   1743, 1898, ☐ , 2098

   (a) 1836   (b) 1899
   (c) 1888   (d) 1829

10. Two children were playing a game using blocks with numbers written on them. A child asked his friend to form the smallest 5-digits odd number with the given blocks.

    | 3 | 0 | 2 | 7 | 6 |

    The number will be
    (a) 02367   (b) 20367
    (c) 30267   (d) 23076

11. Three persons spent ₹ 1072, ₹ 260 and ₹ 128 to buy some household items. If the amounts spent were added, then how many tens are there in the total amount?
    (a) 1   (b) 4
    (c) 6   (d) 2

12. Fill in the blanks and choose the correct option.

(i) 8	(ii) largest
(iii) 13	(iv) 0
(v) smallest	(vi) 2
(vii) cannot be determined	
(viii) 7	

    I. One crore is a/an .... digit number.

    II. The successor of largest 4-digit number is the .... 5-digit number.

    III. .... number has no roman numeral.

IV. Difference between the successor and the predecessor of a number is always ....

	I	II	III	IV		I	II	III	IV
(a)	(vi)	(ii)	(iii)	(vii)	(b)	(i)	(v)	(iv)	(vi)
(c)	(i)	(v)	(iii)	(viii)	(d)	(viii)	(ii)	(iii)	(vii)

13. Which number does the place value of model shows?

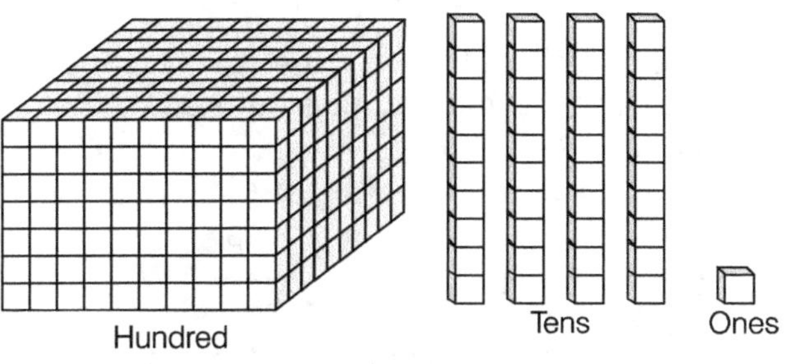

Hundred   Tens   Ones

(a) 121   (b) 740   (c) 141   (d) 741

14. A number contains the digit 4 in it. Which of the following cannot be the number?

(a) 34 tens 47 ones   (b) 42 tens 7 ones
(c) 41 tens 27 ones   (d) 82 tens 22 ones

15. Some roman numbers are given below. Use the sign '>, < or =' to fill the boxes and then choose the correct option that follow.

I.   LIV   ☐   XCIX
II.   XLIV   ☐   XLVI
III.   CCV   ☐   XCV

(a) =, <, <   (b) <, >, =   (c) <, <, >   (d) >, <, >

16. Rounded to the nearest 100, the population of Bolivia was 453400. Which of the following number could be the actual population of Bolivia?

(a) 4500321   (b) 453295
(c) 453364   (d) 4544892

17. A man shows his fingers as shown in the figure. It represents the roman numeral _____ .

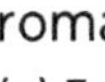

(a) 5   (b) 4
(c) 6   (d) 2

18. The picture given below shows four different magazines. The numeral below each magazine is the total number of copies of the magazine sold last year.

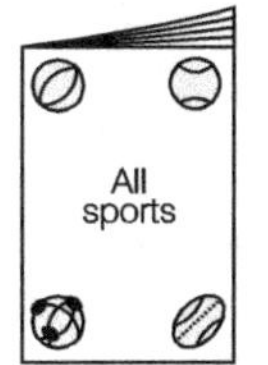

MCCCLIII   MCXXIII   DXXIV   DCCXLVIII

The number of copies sold in which magazine has 4 in tens place?

(a) All sports   (b) Young people
(c) Teenage   (d) Music time

19. Which abacus shows the correct representation of 9243?

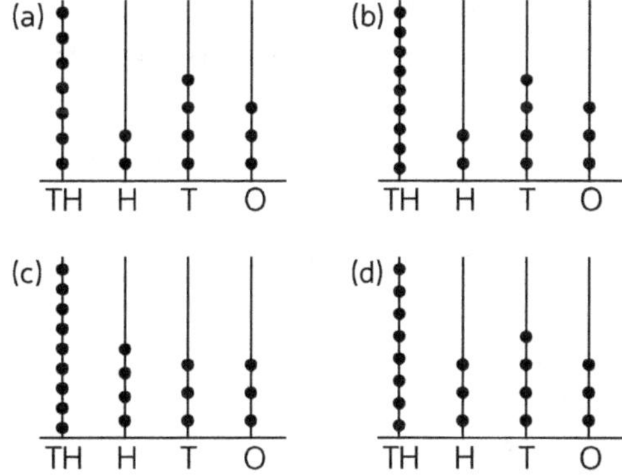

20. Match the following and choose the correct option.

I.	926543	(i)	Smallest 5-digit number
II.	10000	(ii)	Place value of 2 is 2000
III.	962540	(iii)	100039 when rounded off to nearest 100
IV.	100000	(iv)	Successor of 926542

	I	II	III	IV
(a)	(iv)	(i)	(ii)	(iii)
(b)	(ii)	(iii)	(iv)	(i)
(c)	(iv)	(iii)	(ii)	(i)
(d)	(ii)	(i)	(iv)	(iii)

21. Which one of the following digits does not occur in the difference between the successor of 67854398 and the predecessor of 54677456?
(a) 1 (b) 3
(c) 2 (d) 4

22. Ramesh is playing with three cards having numbers written on them. He has to pick the cards in order to make a 3-digit number. Choose the option which shows all the possible combinations of cards.

$$\boxed{9}\ \boxed{4}\ \boxed{7}$$

(a) 947, 749, 497, 794, 479
(b) 974, 749, 794, 799, 947, 977
(c) 749, 797, 479, 497, 974, 947
(d) 947, 974, 479, 749, 794, 497

23. State whether true or false and choose the correct option.

   I. 6380 is 6400 when rounded off to nearest hundred.

   II. Hindu–numeric notation for CCXLV is 265.

   III. Smallest 4-digit number that can be formed by using the digits 3, 5, 8, 0 is 0358.

   IV. Sum of the smallest and largest 4-digit number is 10999.

	I	II	III	IV		I	II	III	IV
(a)	T	T	F	F	(b)	T	F	T	T
(c)	T	F	F	T	(d)	F	T	F	T

24. Jamal's clues about his mystery number are as shown in the box. What is Jamal's mystery number?

My number has

(i) 5 tens	(ii) 8 thousand
(iii) 2 ones	(iv) 6 ten thousand
(v) 0 ones	

(a) 58260 (b) 62850
(c) 68052 (d) 86520

25. Swimming pools at four different schools hold MCCLIII gallons, MMMD gallons, MMMMDXCIV gallons and MMCDXC gallons.

Which inequality correctly compares the number of gallons in two of the pools?
(a) MCCLIII > MMMMDXCIV
(b) MMMD < MCCLIII
(c) MMMMDXCIV < MMCDXC
(d) MMMMDXCIV > MMMD

26. The difference between the smallest and the largest 5-digit number formed by the digits 5, 4, 2, 6, 0 is
(a) 44964 (b) 62964
(c) 46956 (d) 62985

27. $\boxed{986,\ 869,\ 698,\ 896,\ 968,\ 689}$

Calculate the sum of the digits in the hundred place of the smallest and the largest numbers in the above box.
(a) 17 (b) 15
(c) 14 (d) 16

28. What is the difference between the face value and place value of 9 in the number 26594325?
(a) 89991 (b) 9999
(c) 10999 (d) 89982

Direction (Q. Nos. 29-30) The cost of a Book, Hockey stick, Bottle and Paper clip is given.

Book	LXXXVI
Hockey stick	CLV
Bottle	LXVII
Paper clip	XXV

29. Which is the costliest item among all?
(a) Book (b) Hockey stick
(c) Bottle (d) Paper clip

30. What is the total cost of a paper clip, hockey stick and a book?
(a) CCLXVI (b) CXV
(c) CCXLVI (d) CCXLI

Operations on Numbers

As we know about numbers and number system, so now we will study about four basic operations on numbers are addition, subtraction, multiplication and division.

Addition Adding two or more numbers means to find their sum (or total). The symbol used for addition is '+'.

Subtraction Subtraction is the opposite of addition. Subtracting one number from the other means to find the difference between them. The symbol used for subtraction is '−'.

Multiplication Multiplication means repeated addition. The symbol used for multiplication is '×'. A product is the result of the multiplication of two or more numbers.

Division Division can be considered as opposite of multiplication or repeated subtraction. The symbol used for division is '÷'.

Some Important Facts

- ✦ Any number added to 0 is the number itself.
- ✦ Product of any number and zero is zero.
- ✦ If we subtract 0 from any number, the result is the number itself.
- ✦ If we divide any number by itself, the result is always 1.
- ✦ The product of any number multiplied by 1 is the number itself.
- ✦ If we divide any number by 1, then the result is the number itself.

Let's Practice

1. John had 4 bags of pennies as shown below:

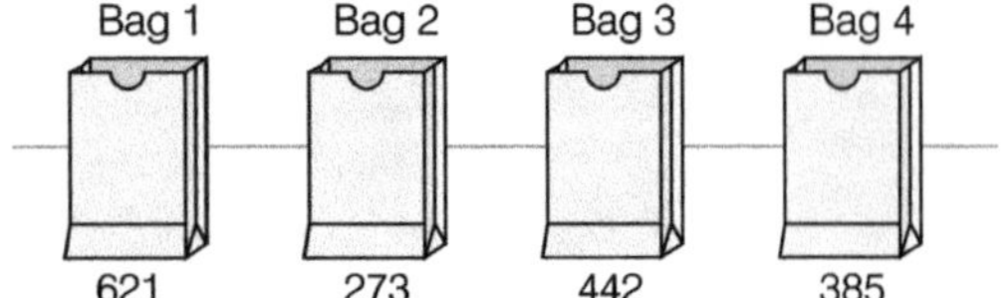

   How many pennies John had in total when rounded off to nearest hundred?
   (a) 1500   (b) 1700   (c) 1600   (d) 1800

2. The sum of two numbers is 17643. One of the number is 6689. Then, the other number is
   (a) 24332   (b) 10954   (c) 65483   (d) 2219

3. Which of the following figure represents 3×4?

   (a) 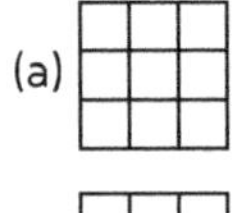   (b) 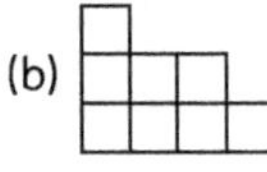

   (c) 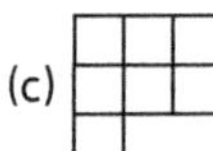   (d) 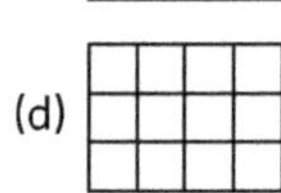

4. 6598 plants were planted in Delhi by some school students on Environment day while 2593 plants were planted in Uttar Pradesh. How many more plants were planted in Delhi than Uttar Pradesh?
   (a) 9191   (b) 4005   (c) 5824   (d) 6695

5. Namita is playing a game in which she multiplies some numbers and get the product. Among the following, choose the option which does not have the product equal to 1144.
   (a) 23×18 (b) 44×26 (c) 52×22 (d) 104×11

6. What is the product of all the numbers on a telephone keypad?
   (a) 158480   (b) 159450   (c) 159480   (d) 0

7. Aman was asked to verify the answer of the given problem. What expression should he use to obtain the dividend again?

   $$7\overline{)188} \quad 26$$

   Remainder $= 6$
   (a) $(6 \times 26) + 7$ (b) $(26 \times 7) + 7$
   (c) $(7 + 26) \times 6$ (d) $(7 \times 26) + 6$

8. Number of men and women in a city is given below.

   Men =

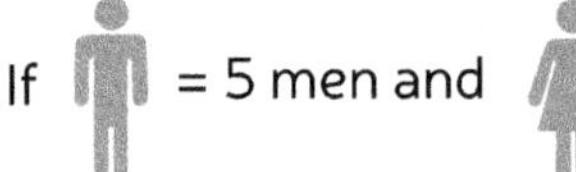 Women = 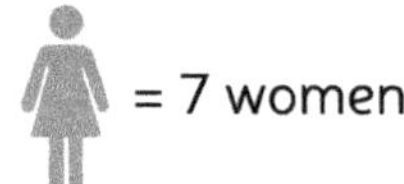

   If = 5 men and = 7 women

   How many women are more than men in the city?
   (a) 5   (b) 1   (c) 6   (d) 3

9. Martin and Louisa bought new sticker books. Martin put 4 stickers in his book everyday and Louisa put 6 stickers in her book everyday. How many stickers will Martin have when Louisa has 30 stickers in her book?

Days	Martin	Louisa
1	4	6
2	8	12
3	12	18

   (a) 16   (b) 20   (c) 24   (d) 36

10. The total number of digits used in numbering 350 pages of the book is
    (a) 959   (b) 924   (c) 900   (d) 942

11. Fill in the blanks and choose the correct option.

(i) one	(ii) minuend
(iii) ten	(iv) zero
(v) number itself	(vi) sum
(vii) product	(viii) subtrahend

    I. The number from which other number is subtracted is called ....

II. No number can be divided by ....

III. When zero is subtracted from a number, the difference is ....

IV. A .... is the result of multiplication of two numbers.

	I	II	III	IV
(a)	(viii)	(iv)	(v)	(vii)
(b)	(ii)	(i)	(iv)	(vi)
(c)	(viii)	(iii)	(v)	(vi)
(d)	(ii)	(iv)	(v)	(vii)

12. The given table shows the marks obtained by Radhika in five subjects out of 50. Which option is closest to the total marks of Radhika in all the five subjects?

Subjects	Marks
A	48
B	36
C	47
D	22
E	37

(a) 165   (b) 200   (c) 250   (d) 300

13. Aryan had 132 tickets. Each ticket can be used by 6 people. How many people can use the tickets?

(a) 610   (b) 792
(c) 685   (d) 22

14. Choose the correct option which makes the given statement true.

I. $94 \times 6 \,\square\, 6 \times 94$

II. $13 \times 9 + 6 \,\square\, 6 \times 9 + 13$

III. $0 \div 83 \,\square\, 83 \div 1$

(a) >, =, =   (b) >, <, <
(c) =, >, <   (d) =, <, =

15. State true or false and choose the correct option.

I. Any number multiplied by 1 is the number itself.

II. $165 + 332 = 332 + 165$

III. Subtraction is the inverse of division.

IV. The number which is subtracted from the other number is called minuend.

	I	II	III	IV
(a)	T	F	T	F
(b)	T	F	F	T
(c)	F	T	F	T
(d)	T	T	F	F

16. Find the value of x.

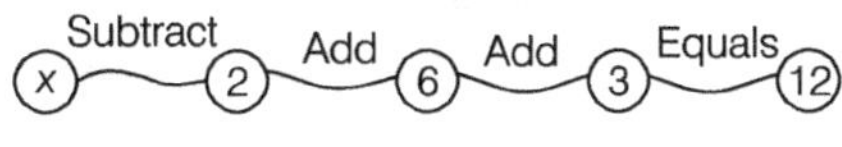

(a) 1   (b) 3
(c) 4   (d) 5

17. There are 534 burgers which are to be packed. 6 burgers can be packed together in 1 packet. How many packets will be needed in all?

(a) 89   (b) 62
(c) 88   (d) 92

18. A tiger eats 9 pounds of flesh in a day. If the tiger caught prey that weighed 315 pounds, how long will the food last?

(a) 35 days   (b) 42 days
(c) 90 days   (d) 82 days

19. In a grazing field, there are 60 goats, 30 deers and 10 children. How many legs are there in the field?

(a) 400   (b) 200   (c) 380   (d) 480

20. Gary has 72 cows on his farm. The number sentence below can be used to find the number of horses, h, Gary has.

$$72 \div h = 6$$

How many horses does Gary have?

(a) 12   (b) 466
(c) 78   (d) 432

21. Find the correct value of the given expression.

$$\text{LIV} \times \text{XXV} = \square$$

(a) MCCCL   (b) MCXL
(c) DCCC   (d) MCCCX

22. I am thinking of a number. If I multiply the number by 85, then add 187 and finally subtract 22, the result is 3735. What number am I thinking of ?

(a) 42   (b) 36   (c) 48   (d) 365

23. Match the following and choose the correct option.

I.	Greatest 3-digit number + 1	(i)	1185 lakh
II.	12 crore − 15 lakh	(ii)	CCLXXVII
III.	135 hundred × 5 hundred	(iii)	M
IV.	CXXXV + CXLII	(iv)	675 ten thousand

```
      I      II     III    IV
(a)  (iii)  (iv)   (i)    (ii)
(b)  (i)    (iii)  (ii)   (iv)
(c)  (iii)  (i)    (iv)   (ii)
(d)  (ii)   (iii)  (iv)   (i)
```

24. The diagram below has some numbers in the boxes. If the sum of numbers in each diagonal is equal, then find the value of A.

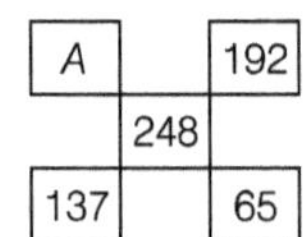

(a) 137 (b) 158
(c) 264 (d) 295

25. Tanvi bought a TV set in exchange of an old fridge. The value of old fridge was ₹ 3250. If she had to pay ₹ 6329, then what was the cost of the TV that Tanvi bought?

(a) ₹ 6329 (b) ₹ 3250
(c) ₹ 9579 (d) ₹ 3079

26. If ❀ + ❀ + ❀ = 6

△ + ❀ + △ = 8

☐ + ☐ = 28

◯ + ◯ + ◯ + ◯ = 64

Then, find the value of

❀ + ❀ + △ + △ + △ + ◯ + ☐

(a) 58 (b) 42
(c) 35 (d) 43

27. If 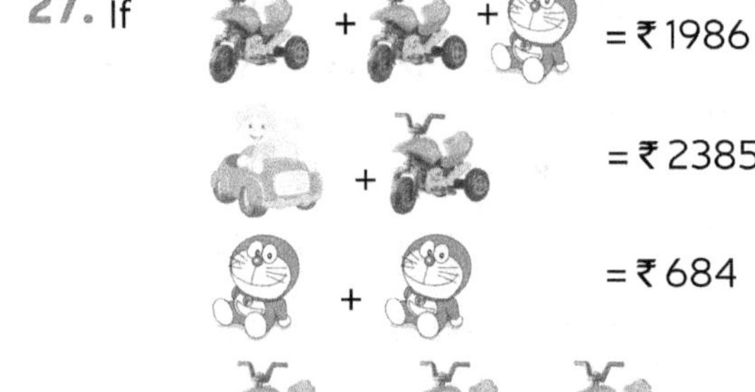 = ₹ 1986

= ₹ 2385

= ₹ 684

Then,

= ?

(a) ₹ 6618 (b) ₹ 5483
(c) ₹ 6495 (d) ₹ 4382

Direction (Q. Nos. 28-29) Study the following example and answer the questions that follow.

$$
\begin{array}{r}
42859 \\
-14X26 \\
\hline
27933 \\
-11Y9 \\
\hline
26774
\end{array}
$$

28. The value of X is
(a) 9 (b) 5
(c) 8 (d) 6

29. The value of Y is
(a) 1 (b) 3
(c) 5 (d) 2

30. Cody is playing a game of darts. The dart board is divided into 3 sections having different points written on it. The score of Cody is the sum of the points he acquires after throwing 3 darts on the board. Which of the following cannot be the score of Cody?

(a) 15 (b) 18
(c) 17 (d) 23

Mathematics Olympiad Class IV

Factors and Multiples

Factors   Factors are the numbers that exactly divide the another number.

e.g.   Factors of 6 are 1, 2, 3 and 6.

Multiples   The product of two numbers is called a multiple of each of the numbers.   e.g 8 and 16 are multiples of 8.

Prime numbers   The numbers who have only two factors, 1 and the number itself are called prime numbers. e.g. 2, 3, 5, 7, 9, 11, etc.

Composite numbers   The numbers who have more than 2 factors are called composite numbers.

e.g.   4, 6, 8, 9, ... etc.

Note   1 is neither a prime number nor a composite number.

Coprime prime numbers   The numbers which have 1 as their common factor are called coprime numbers.

e.g.   2 and 3 are coprime.

Even number   A number which is exactly divisible by 2 is called an even number.

e.g.   2, 4, 6, ... etc.

Odd number   A number which is not exactly divisible by 2 is called an odd number.

e.g.   1, 3, 5, 7, ... etc.

LCM (Least Common Multiple)   The LCM of two or more numbers is the smallest number which is a multiple of each of the given numbers.

HCF (Highest Common Factor)   The HCF of two or more numbers is the largest number which is a factor of each of the given numbers.

Let's Practice

1. Which number is the factor of every number?
   (a) 1
   (b) 0
   (c) Number itself
   (d) None of these

2. Anna collected 8 water bottles. Raj collected twice as many.
   How many water bottles did Raj collect?
   (a) 24   (b) 16   (c) 8   (d) 4

3. Some numbers are shown below :

   | 1, 3, 9, 18, 15, 45, 24, 27, 30, 71 |

   Which of the three numbers shown above are multiples of 9?
   (a) 1, 3, 9
   (b) 18, 45, 24
   (c) 15, 45, 24
   (d) 9, 18, 45

4. The given chart shows the number of pencils students have. Which two students have number of pencils that could be shared equally among three students?

Students	Number of pencils
Prashant	13
Radhika	12
Sonal	19
Neha	15

   (a) Prashant and Radhika
   (b) Radhika and Sonal
   (c) Radhika and Neha
   (d) Sonal and Neha

5. Subtract the sum of the 6th multiple of 7 and the 3rd multiple of 9 from the 11th multiple of 12. The result is
   (a) 60   (b) 50   (c) 63   (d) 70

6. Use the equation given below to answer the question.
   $$14 \times 3 = 42$$
   Which statement correctly interprets the expression?
   (a) 42 is 3 more than 14
   (b) 14 is 3 more than 42
   (c) 14 is 3 times as many as 42
   (d) 42 is 3 times as many as 14

7. Figure below shows the prime factors. Then, the value of x is

   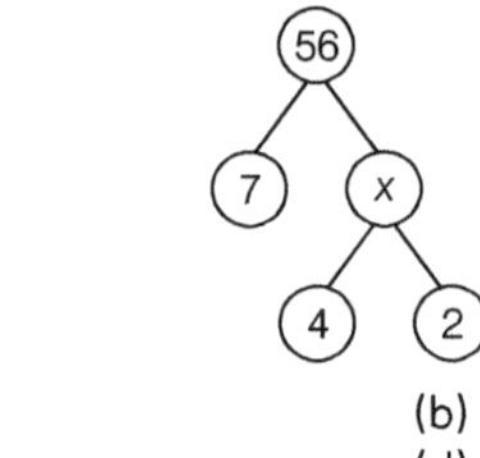

   (a) 8
   (b) 7
   (c) 9
   (d) 5

8. X is a number. X tells I am both factor and multiple of myself. Which one of the following is X?
   (a) 1
   (b) 5
   (c) 7
   (d) All of the above

9. Fill in the blanks and choose the correct option.

(i) 6	(ii) 4
(iii) 2	(iv) 8
(v) 9	(vi) 1
(vii) 7	(viii) 3

   I. .... is the smallest odd prime number.

   II. A number having more than .... factors is called composite number.

   III. .... is neither a prime number nor a composite number.

   IV. The numbers having factors 2 and 3 have factor .... also.

	I	II	III	IV
(a)	(viii)	(iii)	(vi)	(i)
(b)	(iii)	(ii)	(vii)	(iv)
(c)	(vi)	(iii)	(iv)	(viii)
(d)	(ii)	(i)	(vi)	(v)

10. Raghav has the calendar for the month of January in which he has chosen a date for holiday. The date is such that it is a multiple of 7. Also, HCF of the date chosen and the number 24 is 2. What is the date chosen by Raghav?

JANUARY

Sun	Mon	Tue	Wed	Thu	Fri	Sat
						1
2	3	4	5	6	7	8
9	10	11	12	13	14	15
16	17	18	19	20	21	22
23	24	25	26	27	28	29
30	31					

(a) 7   (b) 14   (c) 21   (d) 28

11. The factor of the number shown on abacus is

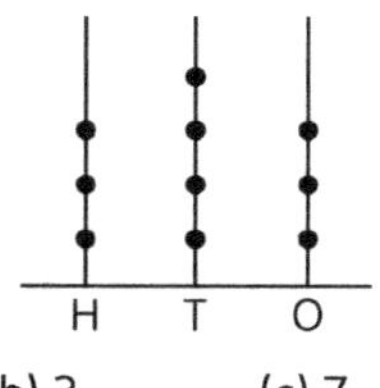

H   T   O

(a) 2   (b) 3   (c) 7   (d) 5

12. State true or false and mark the correct answer.

   I. Two numbers which have only one common factor are called coprime numbers.

   II. 3 is the least prime number.

   III. LCM of two prime numbers is always their product.

   IV. The LCM of any two or more numbers cannot be less than any one of them.

	I	II	III	IV		I	II	III	IV
(a)	T	T	F	F	(b)	T	F	F	T
(c)	T	T	T	F	(d)	T	F	T	T

13. Nisha bought following books from the market which has price written below them. The price of which book is a multiple of 3?

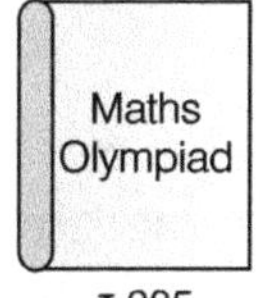

Maths Olympiad	English Olympiad	Computer Olympiad	Science Olympiad
₹ 385	₹ 236	₹ 432	₹ 368

(a) Maths Olympiad   (b) English Olympiad
(c) Computer Olympiad   (d) Science Olympiad

14.   I. X has 2 more factors than 10 has.

   II. X and 10 have 2 common factors.

What is the smallest possible value of X?

(a) 12   (b) 10
(c) 8   (d) 15

15. Here is a sorting diagram with four sections A, B, C and D :

	Multiple of 10	Not a multiple of 10
Multiple of 20	A	B
Not a multiple of 20	C	D

Which of the following numbers can go in section B?

(a) 10   (b) 20   (c) 40   (d) None of these

16. When a number is divided by 5, the quotient is 8 and the remainder is 3. What is the number?

(a) 6th multiple of 7   (b) 4th multiple of 9
(c) Prime number   (d) None of these

17. Lampposts are situated along the roadside at an interval of 8 m. Markings are made on the roadside on every 12 m. How many such markings are made below the lampposts along a 240 m long road?

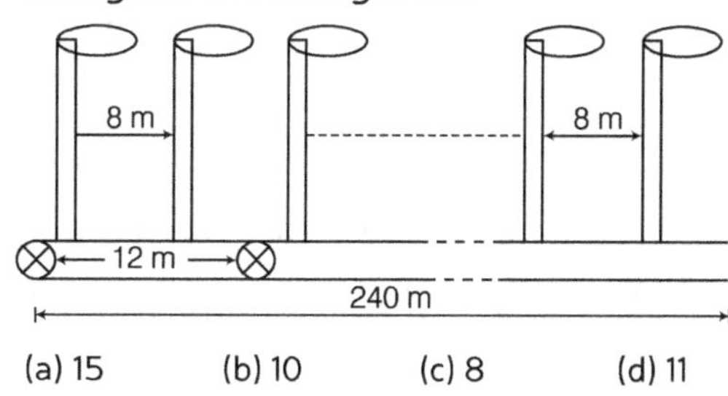

(a) 15   (b) 10   (c) 8   (d) 11

18. In the century (1900-1999), the year which is closest to 21st century and divisible by 2 and 5 both is

(a) 1999   (b) 1990   (c) 1995   (d) 1998

19. Which number am I?

   I. I am a 2-digit even number.

   II. I am a common multiple of 6 and 7.

   III. I have a total of 8 factors.

(a) 43   (b) 35   (c) 42   (d) 84

20. A number is between 20 and 30. It is also a multiple of 4. When it is divided by 8, there is no remainder. What is the number?

(a) 20   (b) 24   (c) 28   (d) 32

21. The smallest number which is a common multiple of 6 and 8, but is not a multiple of 9. When added to 7 fives gives the result as

(a) 80   (b) 60   (c) 59   (d) 65

22. Use the information given below to find the number.

Statement I The number is the predecessor of an even number which is more than 80 but less than 100.

Statement II Number is a multiple of 3.

Statement III Number is not a multiple of 11.

Statement IV Sum of the digits of number is even.

(a) 81   (b) 99
(c) 87   (d) 93

23. Here are steps given to find the greatest number of four digits which is divisible by 15, 25, 40 and 75. Identify the correct order of following steps.

  I. On dividing 9999 by 600, the remainder is 399.

  II. Greatest number of 4 digits is 9999.

  III. LCM of 15, 25, 40 and 75 is 600.

  IV. Number is (9999−399) = 9600.

(a) I   III   II   IV   (b) II   III   I   IV
(c) III   II   IV   I   (d) II   I   III   IV

24. Four students made some statements regarding the numbers given below.

(80) (17) (11) (24)
(40) (2) (48) (84)

Max	There are only 4 multiples of 8.
Jeniffer	Every number is a composite number.
Rocky	(40, 11) are coprime numbers.
Anjie	All the numbers are not even.

Which one of the following made incorrect statement?

(a) Max   (b) Jeniffer   (c) Rocky   (d) Anjie

25. Match the following statements and mark the correct option.

I.	LCM of 15 and 30	(i)	6
II.	LCM of (8, 16)	(ii)	27
III.	Sum of the factors of 2 and 15	(iii)	Factor of 64
IV.	HCF of 24 and 6	(iv)	30

      I   II   III   IV
(a) (i)   (iii)   (iv)   (ii)
(b) (iv)   (iii)   (ii)   (i)
(c) (iii)   (ii)   (i)   (iv)
(d) (iv)   (iii)   (i)   (ii)

Direction (Q. No. 26) Study the given information carefully to answer the following question.

Statement I The smallest three-digit number is the divisor and its successor is the quotient.

Statement II The predecessor of the divisor is the remainder.

26. The dividend is
(a) multiple of 3   (b) multiple of 4
(c) multiple of 7   (d) None of these

27. During summer months, one ice-cream truck visits Jeanette's neighbourhood every 4 days and another ice-cream truck visits her neighbourhood every 5 days. If both trucks visited today, then after how many days will both trucks visit on the same day?

[**Hint** Find the LCM of 4 and 5]
(a) 20   (b) 40
(c) 50   (d) 10

28. Mr. Benrick's family is going to see a hockey match. Entry is ₹ 40 for each child and ₹ 70 for each adult. After buying the tickets Mr. Benrick realised that he spent equal amount of money on buying children's and adults' tickets. What is the minimum equal amount of money he should spent on buying the tickets?

[**Hint** Find the LCM of 40 and 70]
(a) ₹ 70   (b) ₹ 140
(c) ₹ 280   (d) ₹ 320

Direction (Q. Nos. 29-30) Jack bought a rectangular shape drawing paper measuring 42 cm by 27 cm. He wants to cut the drawing paper into as many square shapes as possible with largest length.

29. What is the length of each square?
(a) 5 cm   (b) 4 cm   (c) 3 cm   (d) 8 cm

30. How many such square shape papers can Jack made?
(a) 150   (b) 126   (c) 129   (d) 185

Fractions and Decimals

Fraction

A fraction represents a part of a whole.

Proper fraction   When numerator is less than the denominator, the fraction is called a proper fraction. e.g. $\dfrac{2}{3}, \dfrac{4}{5}$, etc.

Improper fraction   When numerator is greater than denominator, the fraction is called an improper fraction. e.g. $\dfrac{6}{5}, \dfrac{8}{7}$, etc.

Mixed fractions   A combination of a proper fraction and a whole number is called a mixed fraction. e.g. $2\dfrac{1}{2}, 4\dfrac{1}{5}, 6\dfrac{2}{3}$, etc.

Like fractions   The fractions whose denominators are same are called like fractions. e.g. $\dfrac{2}{7}, \dfrac{3}{7}$, etc.

Unlike fractions   The fractions whose denominators are not same are called unlike fractions. e.g. $\dfrac{2}{9}, \dfrac{3}{11}$, etc.

Equivalent fraction   The fractions which have the same value are called equivalent fractions. e.g. $\dfrac{2}{3}, \dfrac{4}{6}, \dfrac{8}{12}$, etc.

Decimal

A decimal is a number written with a decimal point and a remainder that represents a portion of power of ten.

Place value of a decimal   The following chart shows the place value of 4578.925 :

Ten thousands	Thousands	Hundreds	Tens	Ones	and	Tenths	Hundredths	Thousandths	Ten thousandths
	4	5	7	8	•	9	2	5	

Let's Practice

1. There were 15 frogs on a log. 11 hopped away. What fraction of the frogs left behind?

   (a) $\dfrac{11}{15}$ (b) $\dfrac{4}{11}$ (c) $\dfrac{4}{15}$ (d) $\dfrac{15}{4}$

2. Study the figure given below.

   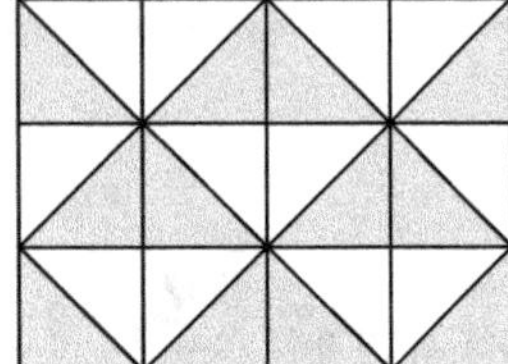

   What fraction of the above figure is shaded?

   (a) $\dfrac{12}{12}$ (b) $\dfrac{6}{12}$ (c) $\dfrac{8}{12}$ (d) $\dfrac{9}{12}$

3. The decimal of shaded part of the figure given below is

   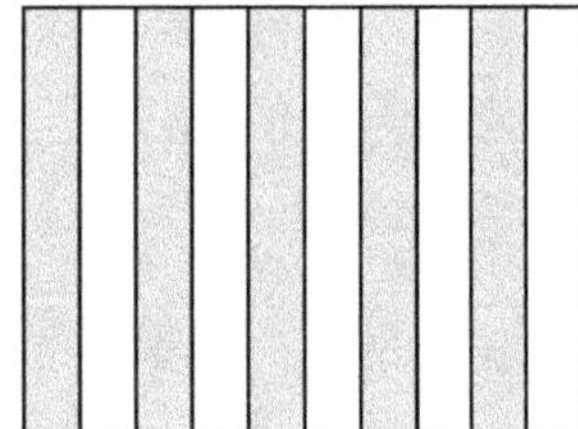

   (a) 0.2   (b) 0.4   (c) 0.3   (d) 0.5

4. Following table shows the match routine of 4 players :

Players	Win	Lost	Matches played
A	4	6	10
B	3	3	6
C	5	7	12
D	8	2	10

   Which player won exactly half the matches he played?

   (a) A   (b) B   (c) C   (d) D

5. **Rama** $=\dfrac{2}{9}$ and $\dfrac{4}{18}$ are equivalent fractions.

   Asha = Two fractions are equivalent when they have same denominators.

   Arjun = Two fractions are equivalent when they have same value.

   Who among them is/are correct?

   (a) Rama and Asha   (b) Asha and Arjun
   (c) Rama and Arjun   (d) All of these

6. Which one of the following fractions does not have the value of numerator 1 less than the denominator?

   (a) $\dfrac{1}{2}+\dfrac{3}{2}$ (b) $\dfrac{2}{5}+\dfrac{2}{5}$

   (c) $\dfrac{7}{9}+\dfrac{1}{9}$ (d) $\dfrac{12}{19}+\dfrac{6}{19}$

7. Which of the following decimals is represented by the given spike abacus?

   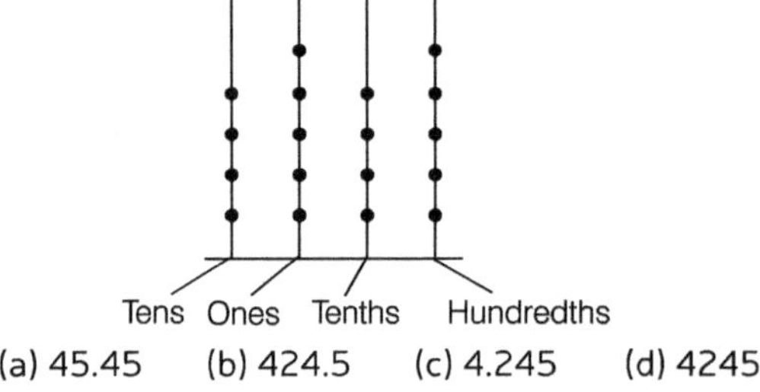

   (a) 45.45   (b) 424.5   (c) 4.245   (d) 4245

8.

   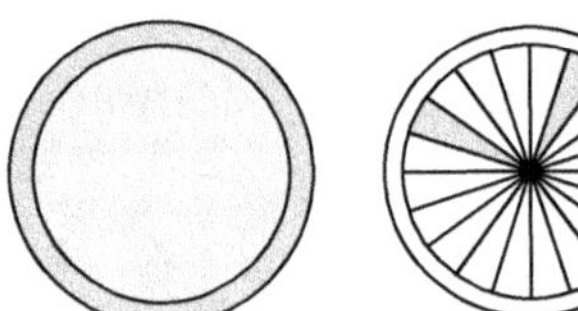

   What decimal fraction does the above picture represent?

   (a) 1.1   (b) 11   (c) 1.3   (d) 13.1

9. There are four companies that built the roads of different lengths as shown in the following table.

	Name of company	Length of road
1.	Max Home	293.50 km
2.	Old Pro Roofing	298.25 km
3.	Constructure Management	293.95 km
4.	Dekenna Development	293.75 km

Mathematics Olympiad Class IV

Which company built the road which is second largest in length?

(a) Max Home

(b) Old Pro Roofing

(c) Constructure Management

(d) Dekenna Development

10. What fraction of alphabets are made of only straight lines?

(a) $\dfrac{15}{26}$ (b) $\dfrac{10}{26}$ (c) $\dfrac{7}{26}$ (d) $\dfrac{18}{26}$

11. What is the value of x, so that the sum of fractions in the diagonal is same?

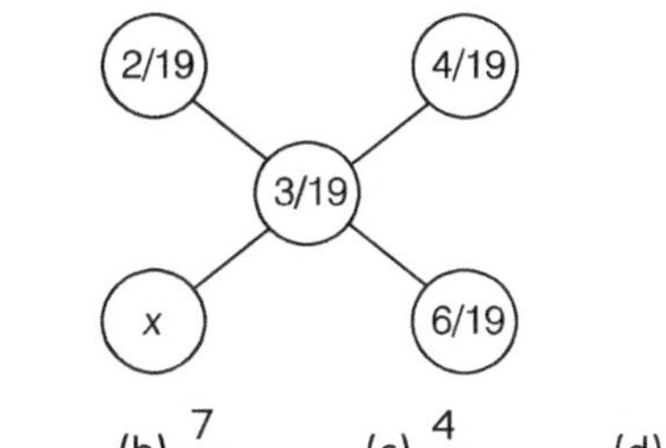

(a) $\dfrac{5}{19}$ (b) $\dfrac{7}{19}$ (c) $\dfrac{4}{19}$ (d) $\dfrac{8}{19}$

12. Which shape does not show one-quarter shaded?

(a) 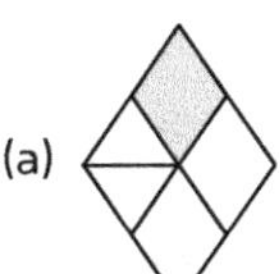   (b) 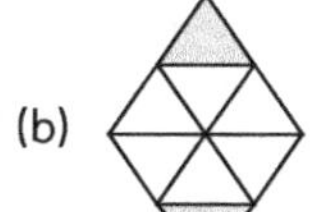

(c) 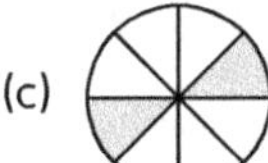   (d) 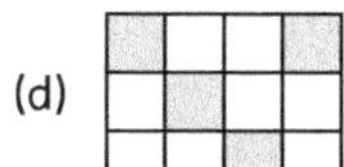

13. Jack is making a chocolate cake and used the ingredients given below.

Ingredients	
$\dfrac{3}{4}$ cup cocoa powder	$\dfrac{1}{2}$ cup butter
2 cup milk	$\dfrac{1}{8}$ cup vanilla essence
$\dfrac{1}{10}$ cup sugar	$\dfrac{3}{4}$ cup cornflour

How many cups of all ingredients did he use to make the chocolate cake?

(a) $\dfrac{135}{15}$ (b) $\dfrac{180}{10}$

(c) $4\dfrac{9}{40}$ (d) $35\dfrac{2}{4}$

14. Given a matrix below which shows two sets of fraction. Each fraction in Ist group is paired with its equivalent fraction in IInd group. Choose a method which should be used to convert the fraction into its equivalent form.

Ist group	$\dfrac{26}{65}$	$\dfrac{104}{117}$	$\dfrac{91}{143}$
IInd group	$\dfrac{2}{5}$	$\dfrac{8}{9}$	$\dfrac{7}{11}$

(a) Add 24 to both numerator and denominator

(b) Subtract 13 from both numerator and denominator

(c) Divide numerator and denominator by 13

(d) Multiply numerator and denominator by 15

15. State whether true or false and choose the correct option.

   I. My glass is half empty, this is same as half full.

  II. I ate half of the chocolate bar. Now, my sister can share it with her friend. They will have one-fourth each.

 III. We have travelled 15 miles already. This is half way, so we have another 20 miles to go.

 IV. I ate three-fourth of pizza, now there are only ten parts of pizza left.

	I	II	III	IV
(a)	F	F	T	T
(b)	T	F	F	T
(c)	T	F	T	F
(d)	T	T	F	F

16. Fill in the place holder with <, > or =

   I. 3.67 ☐ 36.7

  II. 0.25 ☐ 25.0

 III. 3.43 ☐ 3.430

	I	II	III			I	II	III
(a)	<	>	>		(b)	>	>	<
(c)	<	<	=		(d)	>	<	=

17. What is the value of $Q - P$?

(a) $\dfrac{69}{12}$ (b) $\dfrac{17}{10}$ (c) $\dfrac{17}{12}$ (d) $\dfrac{54}{10}$

18. The horses of four cowboys got mixed up. Using conversion of fraction, match the horses with their correct owner.

 $\dfrac{56}{9} \longrightarrow$ (i) 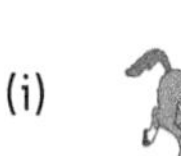 $4\dfrac{1}{9} \longrightarrow$

 $\dfrac{37}{9} \longrightarrow$ (ii)  $2\dfrac{5}{9} \longrightarrow$

 $\dfrac{23}{9} \longrightarrow$ (iii)  $4\dfrac{7}{9} \longrightarrow$

 $\dfrac{43}{9} \longrightarrow$ (iv)  $6\dfrac{2}{9} \longrightarrow$

	I	II	III	IV		I	II	III	IV
(a)	(iii)	(ii)	(i)	(iv)	(b)	(iv)	(i)	(ii)	(iii)
(c)	(ii)	(iii)	(iv)	(i)	(d)	(ii)	(iii)	(i)	(iv)

19. $\dfrac{5}{13}$ and x make two whole. x and $\dfrac{2}{13}$ is $\dfrac{23}{13}$.

What is x?

(a) $\dfrac{21}{13}$ (b) $\dfrac{14}{13}$ (c) $\dfrac{25}{13}$ (d) $\dfrac{5}{13}$

20. Kelly scored 58.93 points and Karen scored 74.92 points in a university exam. How many points less did Kelly scored than Karen?

(a) 14.98 (b) 16.23 (c) 12.24 (d) 15.99

21. Peter has a bamboo rod which has been broken into two pieces. One piece of the rod measure $1\dfrac{1}{5}$ metre and another piece measure $2\dfrac{2}{3}$ metre. What is the total length of the bamboo rod after it has been joined together?

(a) $\dfrac{22}{15}$ metre (b) $\dfrac{58}{15}$ metre

(c) $3\dfrac{1}{15}$ metre (d) $\dfrac{45}{15}$ metre

22. Jimmy is playing a racing game. The fraction below each car shows the time taken by the car to finish the race.

With the help of the time given. Identify the position of cars in which they will finish the race.

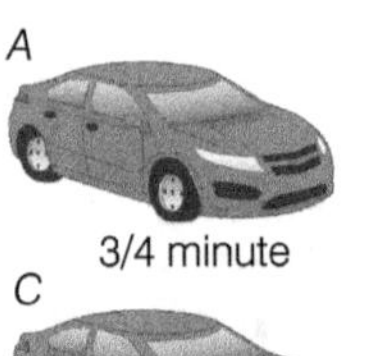

A B

3/4 minute 7/11 minute

C D

7/9 minute 5/7 minute

(a) $C < D < A < B$ (b) $B < C < D < A$
(c) $B < D < A < C$ (d) $A < D < B < C$

23. Select the image from the given options which has the same fraction of unshaded portion as the fraction of the shaded portion of the image below.

(a) 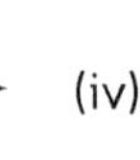 (b) 

(c) (d)

24. The regular price of a meal is ₹ 84. If a coupon is available, how much will the meal price?

$$\boxed{\dfrac{3}{4} \text{ of coupon}}$$

(a) ₹ 21 (b) ₹ 63 (c) ₹ 45 (d) ₹ 70

25. Shalini had 9 apples. $\dfrac{1}{9}$ of her apples she ate on Tuesday and $\dfrac{2}{9}$ she ate on Wednesday and Thursday. The fraction of apples left with her will be

(a) $\dfrac{4}{9}$ (b) $\dfrac{5}{9}$

(c) $\dfrac{1}{9}$ (d) $\dfrac{2}{9}$

26. If the shaded area has a value of $\dfrac{1}{4}$, then the value of the whole shape will be

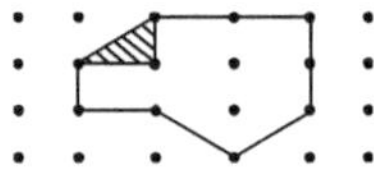

(a) $\dfrac{15}{4}$ (b) $\dfrac{17}{4}$ (c) $\dfrac{19}{4}$ (d) $\dfrac{13}{4}$

Time and Calendar

Time

Time helps us to schedule our daily activities. We check time with the help of a clock. There are 12 numbers written on the face of clock.

A clock consists of two hands Long hand or hour hand and short hand or minute hand.

It is 7 : 30 in the clock. The hour hand is between 7 and 8 and the minute hand is at 6.

The time from 12 mid night to 12 noon is noted as **am** and the time from 12 noon to 12 mid night is noted as **pm**.

→ 1 minute = 60 seconds   → 1 hour = 60 minutes   → 1 day = 24 hours

Calendar

+ A calendar consists of 12 months which constitutes to form 1 year.
+ A year which is divisible by 4 is termed as leap year. There are 366 days in a leap year whereas an ordinary year has 365 days.
+ February is the shortest month of the year. It has only 28 days in an ordinary year and 29 days in a leap year.
+ There are 7 months having 31 days and 4 months having 30 days.
+ 1 week = 7 days
+ 1 year = 12 months

Let's Practice

1. Identify the correct time in the clock.

   (a) 19 : 50   (b) 17 : 45   (c) 18 : 50   (d) 19 : 40

2. On a Sunday morning, it rained from 10 : 07 am till 3 : 15 pm. Calculate the period of rainfall on that Sunday.

   (a) 4 hours 7 minutes   (b) 5 hours 10 minutes
   (c) 5 hours 8 minutes   (d) 5 hours 7 minutes

3. Julia, Kate, Suzanne and Helena wrote down their birthdays on a slip of paper. Kate and Suzanne have their birthdays in the same month. Julia and Suzanne have their birthdays on the same day but not necessarily in the same month.

June	15th
August	3rd
February	21st
June	21st

   Which of the girls was born on August 3rd?

   (a) Julia   (b) Kate   (c) Suzanne   (d) Helena

4. The figure shows the manufacturing and expiry dates of a product.

   For how much time did the product last?

   (a) 2 years   (b) 1 year and 2 months
   (c) 1 year   (d) 2 years and 1 month

5. It is 12 : 53 pm in India. What would be the time in USA, if USA is 15 hours ahead of India?

   (a) 3 : 52 pm (b) 3 : 53 am (c) 12 : 43 am (d) 4 : 53 pm

6. What will be Greenwich mean time, if Indian standard time is 2 : 55 pm?

Indian Standard Time = Greenwich Mean Time + 5 : 30

   (a) 10 : 55 pm   (b) 9 : 25 pm
   (c) 9 : 25 am   (d) 9 : 50 am

7. What is the fraction of the number of days in the month of February in 2012 to the total number of days in that year?

   (a) 29/365   (b) 28/365   (c) 29/366   (d) 28/366

8. If it is Monday on 1st July, then which day of the week will be 15th August?

   (a) Thursday (b) Monday   (c) Friday   (d) Saturday

9. How many minutes should be added to the given time to make it quarter to 5?

   (a) 45 minutes   (b) 40 minutes
   (c) 55 minutes   (d) 25 minutes

10. If Sunrises at 5 : 52 am on a Wednesday morning and there are 13 hours and 32 minutes of day light, then at what time will the sunset?

    (a) 6 : 24 pm (b) 6 : 52 pm (c) 7 : 24 pm (d) 8 : 54 pm

11. Fill in the blanks or choose the correct option.

(i) 7 (ii) am (iii) 4 (iv) mid night (v) 1 (vi) 15 (vii) 5 (viii) pm

    I. An year which is divisible by___is a leap year.

    II. 4 quarter hours =___hour.

    III. There are ___months having 31 days.

    IV. The time from 12 mid night to 12 noon is noted as___.

	I	II	III	IV		I	II	III	IV
(a)	(iii)	(v)	(i)	(ii)	(b)	(vii)	(iii)	(v)	(iv)
(c)	(i)	(iii)	(vii)	(viii)	(d)	(vi)	(vii)	(i)	(iv)

Mathematics Olympiad Class IV

12. Amelie started baking cake. It took 2 hours and 15 minutes to complete it. She completed it at 17:35. At what time did she start baking the cake?

(a) 15 : 20   (b) 16 : 35
(c) 15 : 00   (d) 14 : 20

13. State true or false and mark the correct option.

    I. 3 hours 14 minutes equals 10814 seconds.

    II. 5 : 30 pm or 16 : 30 are same.

    III. 3 hours 49 minutes – 2 hours 58 minutes = 11 minutes.

    IV. 131 hours = 5 days 11 hours.

	I	II	III	IV		I	II	III	IV
(a)	T	T	F	F	(b)	F	F	T	T
(c)	T	F	T	F	(d)	F	F	F	T

14. The diagram below shows the travelling time of Michael from house to school and school to garden. If it is 6:20 am now, then at what time will he reach the garden, if he starts travelling from his home?

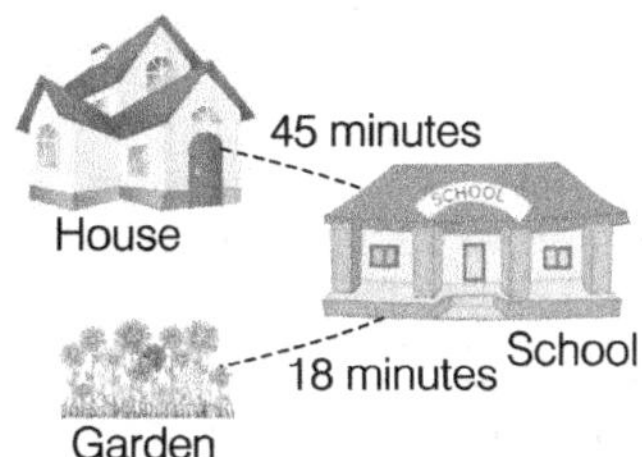

(a) 7 : 10 am   (b) 6 : 55 am
(c) 7 : 15 am   (d) 7 : 23 am

15. Match the analog clock with digital clock.

A.		1.	23 : 55
B.		2.	8 : 50
C.		3.	13 : 20
D.		4.	18 : 30

	A	B	C	D		A	B	C	D
(a)	3	2	1	4	(b)	4	2	3	1
(c)	4	3	2	1	(d)	2	3	4	1

16. Sally got her new phone 1 week and 5 days before from today. If she got the phone on January 15th. What is the date today?

January						
Sun	Mon	Tue	Wed	Thu	Fri	Sat
		1	2	3	4	5
6	7	8	9	10	11	12
13	14	15	16	17	18	19
20	21	22	23	24	25	26
27	28	29	30	31		

(a) 27th January   (b) 22nd January
(c) 28th January   (d) 26th January

17. Zane found a page from 2008 calendar. He found a note on the page.

> I am going for shopping on the last Saturday of May. Six days later, I am going to UK.
>   David

May 2008						
Sun	Mon	Tue	Wed	Thu	Fri	Sat
				1	2	3
4	5	6	7	8	9	10
	12	13	14	15	16	17

When did David go to UK?

(a) 30th May, 2008   (b) 5th June, 2008
(c) 1st June, 2008   (d) 6th June, 2008

18. Edda's birthday falls on 12th June. If it is Monday on 28th March, 2015, then on what day will be her birthday in the same year?

(a) Monday   (b) Saturday
(c) Sunday   (d) Friday

19. Jessica arrived at the nursery at 8 : 12 am on Tuesday morning. How many minutes did she have to wait for the nursery to open?

Market of plants

Days	Open	Close
Monday	9 : 00 am	6 : 00 pm
Tuesday	8 : 30 am	5 : 30 pm
Wednesday	8 : 30 am	6 : 00 pm
Thursday	8 : 00 am	5 : 00 pm
Friday	10 : 00 am	6 : 30 pm

(a) 54 minutes   (b) 30 minutes
(c) 16 minutes   (d) 18 minutes

20. In a game of 'spinning the wheel', it takes about 2 seconds for the pin in going from one month to the next month in anti-clockwise direction. If the wheel spins for about 30 seconds, then at which month the pin of the wheel stops?

(a) March

(b) February

(c) November

(d) January

21. A traffic light changes its colour after every 2 minutes in the order as follows

$$red \rightarrow yellow \rightarrow green$$

If it is red now and time is 5 : 20 pm, then at what time light becomes green, if it stopped working for 25 minutes?

(a) 5 : 40 pm (b) 5 : 50 pm (c) 5 : 49 pm (d) 5 : 47 pm

22. A train which was scheduled to come at Shahdra station got 1 hour 15 minutes late. It leaves the station after 10 minutes and reach Ajmer station at 6 : 00 pm after 8 hours of journey.

The train scheduled time to arrive at Shahdra station is

(a) 8 : 35 am (b) 9 : 00 am (c) 10 : 35 am (d) 10 : 00 am

23. Sara takes the piano lessons every third day. If she marks on the calendar her first lesson in March, then on which of the following day in March, Sara will not have any class?

March						
Mon	Tue	Wed	Thu	Fri	Sat	Sun
			1	2	3	4
5	6	7	8	9	10	11
12	13	14	15	16	17	18
19	20	21	22	23	24	25
26	27	28	29	30	31	

(a) Monday

(b) Friday

(c) Tuesday

(d) Thursday

24. I was flying from London to Sydney with no stop overs. I left London at 2 : 20 pm Tuesday and arrived in Sydney at 6 : 40 pm Wednesday. How long was the flight, if Sydney is 11 hours ahead of London?

(a) 17 hours

(b) 17 hours 20 minutes

(c) 15 hours

(d) 18 hours 40 minutes

25. Brenda's clock is set 20 minutes ahead of the actual time. The alarm goes off when the clock reads 5 : 30 am. Each time she hits the snooze button, the alarm waits 7 minutes, then rings again. She gets up when the alarm rings for the third time. What is the actual time when she gets up?

(a) 5 : 51 am

(b) 5 : 36 am

(c) 5 : 24 am

(d) 5 : 15 am

Money

Money is a medium of exchange in the form of coins and banknotes.

India's unit to measure money is rupee. The symbol for rupee is '₹'.

1 rupee = 100 paise	75 paise = 3/4 rupee
50 paise = 1/2 rupee	25 paise = 1/4 rupee

Addition and subtraction of money Money is added and subtracted in the same way as we add whole numbers and decimal numbers and put the sign of rupees before the answer.

Example 1   Add ₹ 14.75 and ₹ 12.24.

Sol.
$$\begin{array}{r} ₹\ 14.75 \\ +\ ₹\ 12.24 \\ \hline ₹\ 26.99 \\ \hline \end{array}$$

Example 2   Subtract ₹ 2.95 from ₹ 6.42.

Sol.
$$\begin{array}{r} ₹\ 6.42 \\ -\ ₹\ 2.95 \\ \hline ₹\ 3.47 \\ \hline \end{array}$$

Conversion from rupees to paise and from paise to rupees Conversion from rupees to paise and paise to rupees is based on the basic fact that ₹ 1 = 100 paise and 100 paise = ₹ 1.

Example 1   Convert ₹ 5 to paise.

Sol. ∵ ₹ 1 = 100 paise

∴ ₹ 5 = 5 × 100 paise = 500 paise

Example 2   Covert 900 paise into rupees.

Sol. ∵ 100 paise = ₹ 1

∴ 900 paise = ₹ 900 ÷ 100 = ₹ 9

Let's Practice

1. $\frac{1}{4}$ of x rupees is equal to 25 paise, then the value of x is

   (a) ₹ 1   (b) ₹ 2   (c) ₹ 25   (d) ₹ 3

2. ₹ 7.00 = $x \times 50$ paise, then the value of x is

   (a) 10   (b) 14   (c) 20   (d) 24

3. Which of the following has the least value?

   (a) 280 paise   (b) ₹ 4.85

   (c) 5 × 25 paise   (d) Twenty 10 paise coins

4. Jack lives in Ottawa, Canada. His uncle lives in London, England. On his birthday, Jack received £ 20 from his uncle. How many canadian dollars can he buy with his birthday money? (£ 1 = $ 1.74)

   (a) $ 35.23   (b) $ 34.65   (c) $ 39.28   (d) $ 34.80

5. What is the choice of coins you may use for paying ₹ 9.25?

   (a) four 2 rupee coins, one 1 rupee coin and one 25 paise coins
   (b) four 2 rupee coins, one 50 paise coin and one 25 paise coin
   (c) one 5 rupee coin and twelve 50 paise coins
   (d) one 5 rupee coins, two 1 rupee coins and six 25 paise coins

6. State true or false and choose the correct option.

   I. Thirty five rupees twenty five paise is equal to 35.25.

   II. ₹ 5.75 means five hundred seventy five rupees.

   III. The number of 25 paise coins in ₹ 100 is 40.

   IV.

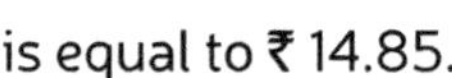

   is equal to ₹ 14.85.

	I	II	III	IV		I	II	III	IV
(a)	T	F	F	F	(b)	T	T	F	F
(c)	T	F	F	T	(d)	T	F	T	F

7. A cricket bat costs ₹ 180. If Bunny has ₹ 500 note, then how much money will he get back?

   (a) ₹ 400   (b) ₹ 360   (c) ₹ 320   (d) ₹ 340

8. Andy made bouquet of flowers containing 10 flowers each. He sold the bouquet at ₹ 50. If he had total of 600 flowers. How much did he get in all?

   (a) ₹ 3000   (b) ₹ 2500
   (c) ₹ 4000   (d) ₹ 2000

9. Fill in the blanks and choose the correct option.

(i) 30	(ii) 300
(iii) 5	(iv) 50
(v) 10	(vi) 250
(vii) 280	(viii) 75

   I. 500 paise makes .... rupees.

   II. .... paise makes two and a half rupee.

   III. $\frac{3}{4}$ of 1 rupee = ... paise

   IV. If the cost of 1 cup of tea is ₹ 6, then cost of 5 cups of tea is ₹ ....

	I	II	III	IV		I	II	III	IV
(a)	(v)	(vii)	(iii)	(ii)	(b)	(iii)	(vi)	(i)	(viii)
(c)	(vi)	(i)	(iii)	(iv)	(d)	(iii)	(vi)	(viii)	(i)

Direction (Q. Nos. 10-11) A college library has the following fine charges for delay in returning of a book.

First day	₹ 1
Second day	₹ 1
Third day	₹ 2
Fourth day	₹ 3
Successive days	₹ 5

If the book is lost or tear, then students have to pay the double price of the book.

10. Kathlean borrowed a book from library and returned it after four days of date of returning. How much fine does Kathlean has to submit to library?

   (a) ₹ 5   (b) ₹ 6   (c) ₹ 7   (d) ₹ 8

11. If Kathlean lost the book, then how much amount will librarian charge, if the cost of book is ₹ 192.65?

(a) ₹ 385.30

(b) ₹ 354.28

(c) ₹ 122.85

(d) ₹ 659.23

12. Christina earns ₹ 100 for every hour as a tuition fees. Last week she worked for 15 hours. She spent 1/ 4 th of the money she earned. How much money is left with her?

(a) ₹ 1000   (b) ₹ 1125

(c) ₹ 1250   (d) ₹ 1025

13. Study the information given below :

 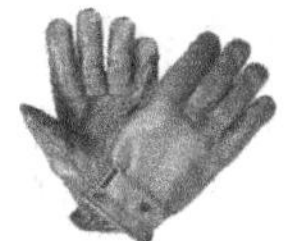  

| ₹ 200 | ₹ 450 | ₹ 50 | ₹ 75 |

Which of the following statement is correct?

(a) Anna has ₹ 100 by which she can buy a bow and a winter cap

(b) Alan has ₹ 250 by which he can buy a pair of gloves

(c) Suzanne is carrying ₹ 500 and she can buy two bows, a winter cap and a purse

(d) None of the above

14. Match the following and mark the correct option.

List I	List II
I. ₹ 48 ÷ ₹ 3	(i) ₹ 4
II. 16 × 25 paise	(ii) ₹ 16
III. ₹ 23.25 – ₹ 6.95	(iii) ₹ 19.40
IV. ₹ 19.65 – 25 paise	(iv) ₹ 16.30

	I	II	III	IV
(a)	(ii)	(iii)	(iv)	(i)
(b)	(ii)	(ii)	(i)	(iv)
(c)	(iii)	(iv)	(ii)	(i)
(d)	(ii)	(i)	(iv)	(iii)

15. Which of the following is a better buy?

(a) 2 candy bars for ₹ 5.90

(b) 6 candy bars for ₹ 19.5

(c) 4 candy bars for ₹ 4.76

(d) Cannot be determined

16. Compare using <, > or =.

I. 560 paise ☐ ₹ 7.80.

II. $\frac{2}{3}$ of ₹ 9 ☐ 600 paise

III. 7 one rupee note ☐ 10 fifty paise coins.

IV. 6 rupees and 25 paise ☐ 5 rupees and 200 paise.

	I	II	III	IV		I	II	III	IV
(a)	<	>	=	<	(b)	>	=	>	>
(c)	>	<	<	>	(d)	<	=	>	<

17. Hannu wants to buy a video game whose price is ₹ 150. He decided to save ₹ 20 in first week, ₹ 40 in second week ₹ 60 in third week and so on. After how many weeks will he be able to buy the video game?

Number of weeks	Savings	Total
1	₹ 20	₹ 20
2	₹ 40	₹ 60
3	₹ 60	₹ 120
⋮	⋮	⋮

(a) 5   (b) 3   (c) 6   (d) 4

18. Kia has some notes which consists of ₹ 1, ₹ 10 and ₹ 50 notes. If her savings is ₹ 415 and he has four ₹ 10 notes and twenty five ₹ 1 note, then how many notes of ₹ 50 he has?

(a) 7   (b) 8   (c) 6   (d) 9

19. After purchasing 5 pens for ₹ 17.75 each Stella has ₹ 15.95 left. How much money she had at first?

(a) ₹ 88.75   (b) ₹ 109.50

(c) ₹ 104.70   (d) ₹ 95.95

20. Tessie, Adira and Tulip wants to clean out junk. Tessie has 15 kg newspaper, Adira has 13 kg plastic whereas Tulip has 2 kg iron and 4 kg brass. They all went to Ragman whose price list is as shown.

Ragman Price List	
Kinds of Junk	**Price of 1 kg**
1. Newspaper	₹ 6/-
2. Iron	₹ 14/-
3. Brass	₹ 180/-
4. Plastic	₹ 12/-
5. Waste paper	₹ 4.50/-

Which of the following statement is correct?
(a) Ragman pay ₹ 90 to Adira
(b) Tulip will get ₹ 784 in return for her junk
(c) Amount received by Tessie and Adira is more than the amount received by Tulip
(d) Total money which Ragman had to pay to all the three women is ₹ 994

21. Rex hired a taxi. It charges ₹ 8 for the first kilometre and ₹ 10 for the successive kilometres. How much money Rex had to pay, if he travelled 58 km?
(a) ₹ 472　　　　(b) ₹ 590
(c) ₹ 500　　　　(d) ₹ 588

22. 

If the price of one shirt is ₹ 175.75, then how many shirts can I get for ₹ 754.50 with the offer as shown above?
(a) 6　　　　(b) 10
(c) 8　　　　(d) 9

23. Joshie paid a total of ₹ 572 for 4 toy cars and 6 cookies. Each toy car costs ₹ 38 more than a cookie. What is the cost of each cookie?
(a) ₹ 42　　　　(b) ₹ 56
(c) ₹ 38　　　　(d) ₹ 59

24. Four friends are going to watch a movie. The ticket cost ₹ 200 per person and have $\frac{1}{4}$th off on girls entry. They spent ₹ 200 on food and ₹ 50 as travelling charges. If the money was divided equally among them, then what was the share of each?

(a) ₹ 750　　　　(b) ₹ 625.95
(c) ₹ 237.50　　　　(d) ₹ 500

25. Ann went to spain on a holiday and changes ₹ 280000 to euros. She spent € 450 in spain and from there she went to meet his brother who lives in France. There she spent \$352 and returned to India. How much money she is left with?
(\$1 = ₹ 62.5, ₹ 1 = € 0.014 and € 1 = \$ 1.13)
(a) ₹ 235960.25　　　　(b) ₹ 223068.75
(c) ₹ 219582. 95　　　　(d) ₹ 245923.12

Measurement

Measurement is defined as the act of measuring the size of something.

Metric system is widely used in different countries for measurement.

Length   As per the metric system, the fundamental or base unit for length is metre.

+ Length is most commonly measured in millimetre, centimetre, metre and kilometre.
+ Small units of length are measured in millimetre.
+ 10 equal parts of millimetre together makes 1 cm i.e. 10 mm = 1cm
+ Larger distances are usually measured in kilometre.
+ 1000 equal parts of metre together makes 1 km i.e. 1000 m = 1 km

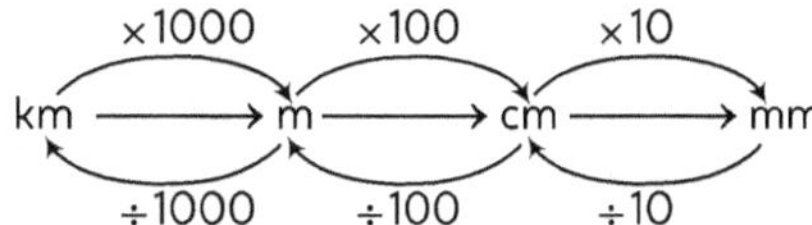

Weight (Mass)   As per the metric system, the fundamental unit for mass is kilogram.

+ The three most common units of measuring mass are gram, kilogram and milligram.
+ Lighter objects are measured in gram and milligram.
+ Heavier objects are measured in kilogram.
+ 1000 equal parts of gram together makes 1 kg i.e. 1000 g = 1 kg

Volume   As per the metric system, fundamental unit for measuring capacity or volume is litre.

+ The most common units of measuring volume are litre and millilitre.
+ Smaller quantities or volume are measured in millilitre.
+ Larger quantities are measured in litre.

$$1 \text{ litre (L)} = 1000 \text{ millilitre (mL)}$$

Let's Practice

1. The correct arrangement of the following items in order of which holds the least to which holds the most will be

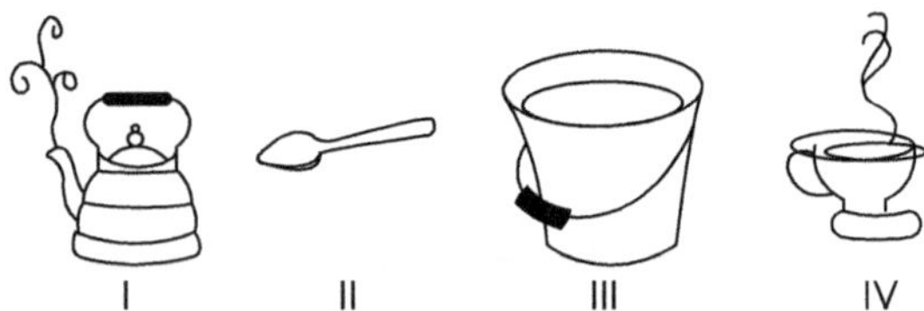

(a) II < I < III < IV
(b) II < IV < III < I
(c) II < I < IV < III
(d) II < IV < I < III

2. Which of the following should not be measured in litre or millilitre?

orange juice, petrol, potatoes, milk

(a) Orange juice
(b) Petrol
(c) Potatoes
(d) Milk

3. The correct measure of the object to nearest millimetre is

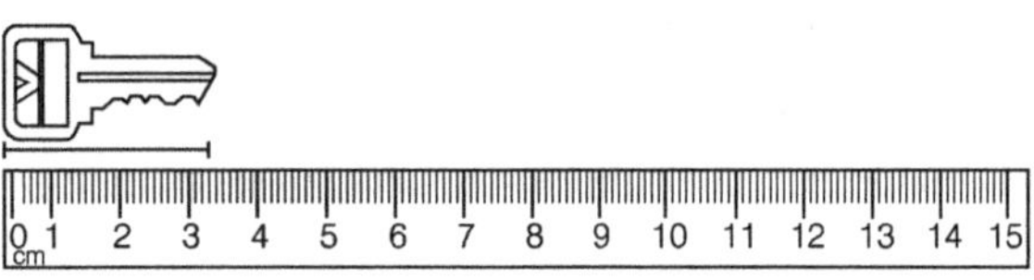

(a) 3.4 cm   (b) 3.2 cm   (c) 3.3 cm   (d) 3.5 cm

4. Four statements are given below. State which of them is true or false and choose the correct option.

I. Very short lengths are measured (in millimetre).

II. Long distances are measured (in metre).

III. In 1 m, there are 0.001 km.

IV. You can fill 5 glasses of 200 mL from a jug containing 1 L milk.

	I	II	III	IV
(a)	F	T	F	T
(b)	T	F	T	T
(c)	T	F	T	F
(d)	T	T	F	T

5. Match the following with the most appropriate instrument of measurement and choose the correct option.

I.	Length of football field	(i)
II.	Weight of a kilogram of meat	(ii)
III.	Length of a paper clip	(iii)
IV.	Volume of milk	(iv)

	I	II	III	IV
(a)	(ii)	(iii)	(iv)	(i)
(b)	(ii)	(iv)	(i)	(iii)
(c)	(ii)	(iii)	(i)	(iv)
(d)	(iv)	(ii)	(i)	(iii)

6. Kacy is preparing for a test on measurement. Her mother gives her four statements out of which one is incorrect. Identify the incorrect statement.

I. Length of a street can be between 2 km and 4 km.

II. 7 kg = 7200 g − 200 g

III. Volume of eye drops is measured in millilitre.

IV. Decagram is a bigger unit than hectogram.

(a) I   (b) II
(c) III   (d) IV

7. If each part on the number line is of 1 cm.

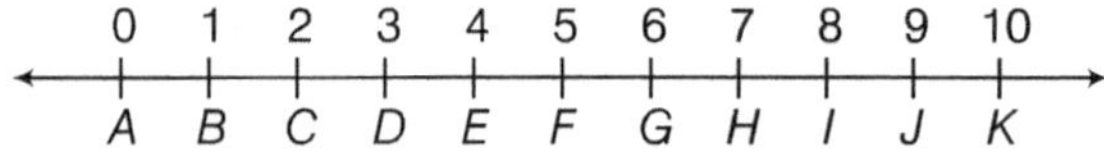

Then, sum of $AD + EF + HJ$ is

(a) AF (b) DJ
(c) CG (d) EJ

8. Fill the missing sign and choose the correct option.

   I. 8 ☐ 1000 g = 8 kg

   II. 900 ☐ 100 g = 1 kg

   III. 4000 g ☐ 4 = 1 kg

   IV. 780 g ☐ 280 g = 0.5 kg

(a) ×, +, ÷, −   (b) ×, ÷, +, −   (c) ÷, ×, +, −   (d) ÷, +, − +

9. Moishe has a can of lemonade containing 400 mL. He drinks $\frac{1}{4}$ of it. How much lemonade is left?

(a) 200 mL   (b) 100 mL   (c) 300 mL   (d) 250 mL

10. Fill in the blanks and choose the correct option.

(i) metre	(ii) 1 g
(iii) 100 g	(iv) litre
(v) milligram	(vi) millimetre
(vii) 1000	(viii) 10

   I. The standard unit of volume or capacity is ______ .

   II. 1000 mg = ______ .

   III. Very light weights are measured in ___ .

   IV. 1 km is ______ times 100 cm.

	I	II	III	IV
(a)	(v)	(iii)	(i)	(vii)
(b)	(iv)	(ii)	(v)	(vii)
(c)	(i)	(vii)	(vi)	(ii)
(d)	(iv)	(iii)	(vi)	(viii)

11. A horse(s) height is measured in a unit called hand. A hand measures 4 inch. What is the height (in inch) of a horse that measures 14 hands?

(a) 36 inch   (b) 46 inch   (c) 56 inch   (d) 66 inch

12. The given diagram shows a weighing balance. 1st pan consists of weights worth 750 g and 2nd pan consists of 2 kg flour. How much weight is needed to add to 1st pan, so that the scales become balanced?

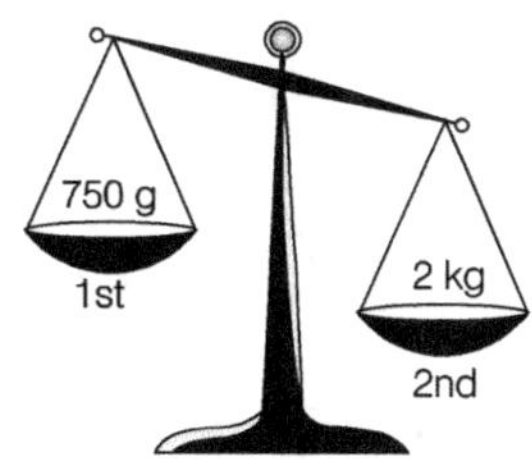

(a) 1250 g   (b) 1000 g   (c) 1500 g   (d) 1325 g

13. Aaron is going to his grandma's house. The distance between Aaron's and his grandma's house is as shown below. Due to wear and tear of the road, Aaron has to take the long route which is about 9.2 km. How much more distance Aaron has to travel in order to reach his grandma's house?

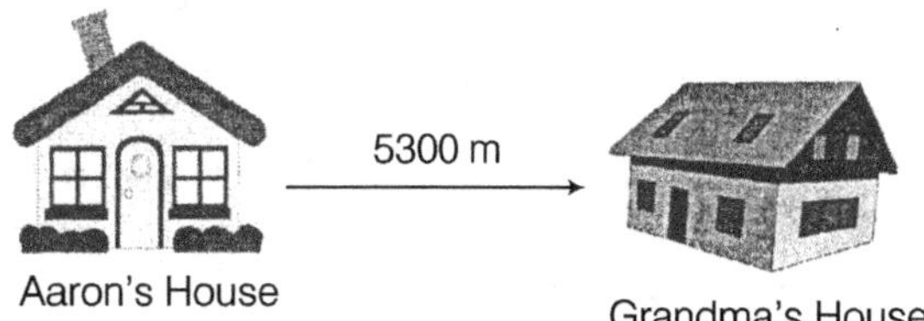

(a) 2.7 km   (b) 3.9 km
(c) 4.8 km   (d) 4.5 km

14. 

A doctor has syrup bottle which is to be given equally to the patients as shown in the diagram. How much syrup will be given to each patient?

(a) 90 mL   (b) 82 mL
(c) 85 mL   (d) 63 mL

15. Krista has 1.5 kL of water in a tank. To empty the tank, she took a 125 L bucket and started watering the plants. How many free buckets will it take to remove all the water from the tank?

(a) 15   (b) 18   (c) 20   (d) 12

16. If the length of rope needed to make border X is 16 cm, then the length of rope needed for border Y

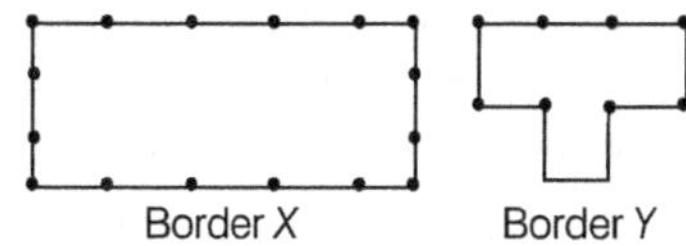

(a) 9 cm   (b) 12 cm   (c) 10 cm   (d) 13 cm

17. Kelsey's pencil box is 16 cm long. Hanna's pencil box is 4 cm shorter than Kelsey's. Mark's pencil box is 2 cm longer than Hanna's. How much long is Mark's pencil box?

(a) 12 cm   (b) 14 cm   (c) 10 cm   (d) 16 cm

18. Danny goes to his office daily by his car. Depending upon the traffic on the road, he requires petrol as given below

Monday	240 mL
Tuesday	560 mL
Wednesday	385 mL
Friday	358 mL
Saturday	237 mL

How much petrol would he need on Thursday, if he required 2180 mL of petrol is entire week?

(a) 500 mL   (b) 400 mL   (c) 40 mL   (d) 600 mL

19. Smith is taking part in an olympic race. The length of each of his step is given in the figure. Calculate how many miles can he run, if he took 20000 steps in the race? (given, 1 mile = 1.6 km)

(a) 9.468 miles   (b) 9.32 miles
(c) 9.375 miles   (d) 10.459 miles

20. The weight of 3 books and a puppy is 12 kg. What is the weight of a book?

(a) 6 kg   (b) 2 kg   (c) 4 kg   (d) 5 kg

21. 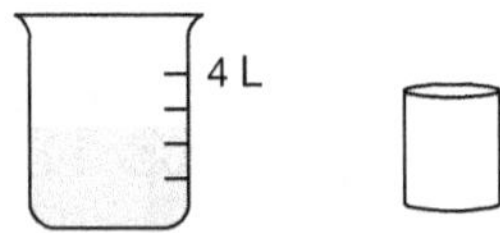

The jug shown here can be filled upto half way mark by pouring 10 full cups of water from a measuring cup into it. How much water does the cup hold when it is full?

(a) 200 mL   (b) 250 mL   (c) 300 mL   (d) 350 mL

22. If 🍎 + 🍎 = 20 g

🍎 + 🍎 + 🍅 = 46 g

🍎 + 🍅 = 24 g

Then, the value of 🍅 is

(a) 10 g   (b) 6 g
(c) 12 g   (d) 8 g

23. A bridge is 600 m long and a truck is 5 m long. How many trucks can stand on this bridge, if the trucks stands with a gap of 1 m?

(a) 150   (b) 120
(c) 100   (d) 130

24. A gift 38 cm long is to be wrapped with a wrapping paper. The length of wrapping paper is 64 cm. A margin of 5 cm on each side is to be taken for folding purpose. How much length of wrapping paper will be left after wrapping the gift?

(a) 21 cm
(b) 16 cm
(c) 26 cm
(d) 20 cm

25. Four bottles contain oil whose volume is shown in the following table. Which two bottles together contain volume less than 4 L 400 mL.

A	3 L 400 mL
B	1 L 650 mL
C	3 L 925 mL
D	2 L 692 mL

(a) A and B   (b) B and C
(c) B and D   (d) C and A

26. Given,

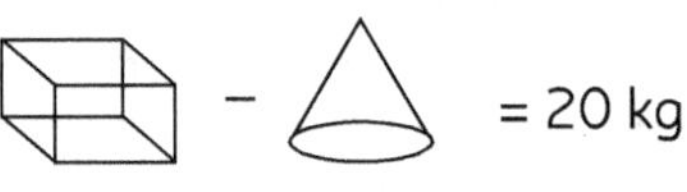

If total weight of

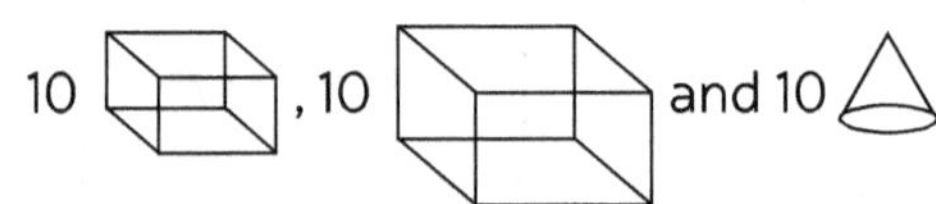

is 3200 g,

then what1 is the weight of ⌂ ?

(a) 140 g   (b) 100 g
(c) 70 g   (d) 30 g

Mathematics Olympiad Class IV

Geometry

Parallel lines Two lines which never meet in a plane are called parallel lines.

Intersecting lines When two lines meet in a plane, then they are called intersecting lines.

Angle Two rays with the same end point is an angle.

Acute angle An angle whose measure is less than 90° is an acute angle.

Right angle An angle whose measure is 90° is a right angle.

Obtuse angle An angle whose measure is greater than 90° but less than 180° is an obtuse angle.

Polygon Any closed figure made up of straight lines is called a polygon. The list of polygon with their number of sides is given below :

Polygons	Sides
Triangle	3
Quadrilateral	4
Pentagon	5
Heptagon	6

Rectangle A quadrilateral whose opposite sides are parallel and equal is called a rectangle.

Square A square is a quadrilateral whose all sides are equal.

Rectangle and square are the types of a quadrilateral.

Circle A circle is a closed geometrical figure formed by points equidistant from a fixed point.

Let's Practice

1. How many line segments are there in the given figure?

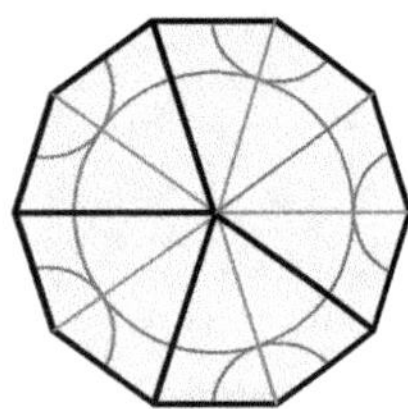

(a) 15   (b) 10   (c) 20   (d) 12

2. Which of the following is an example of a ray?

(a) Tip of a pencil   (b) Equator line
(c) Flashlight   (d) Edges of paper

3. The angle between prime Meridian and the axis of the Earth is a/an

(a) acute angle   (b) obtuse angle
(c) right angle   (d) None of these

4. The number of circles in the given figure is

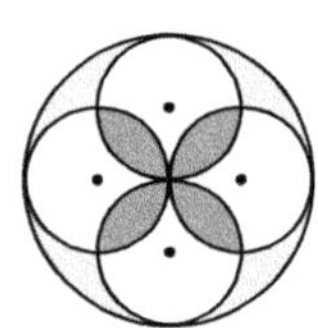

(a) 3   (b) 6   (c) 4   (d) 5

5. Following figure show three clocks showing different times.

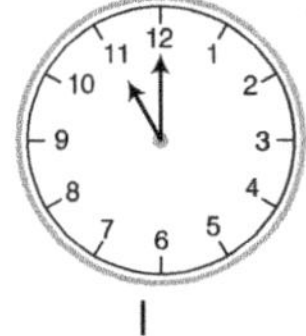  

I   II   III

The angle between the hands of the clock is

	I	II	III
(a)	Obtuse	Acute	Right
(b)	Acute	Right	Obtuse
(c)	Acute	Obtuse	Right
(d)	Right	Obtuse	Acute

6. A polygon with minimum number of sides is called a ______ .

(a) rectangle   (b) square
(c) triangle   (d) circle

7. The picture below shows a tile on the side of a swimming pool.

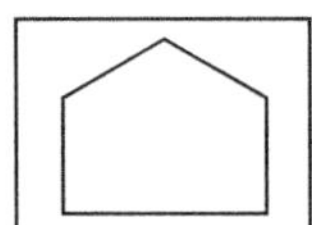

Which of the following options best describes the given shape?

(a) A hexagon inside a square
(b) A square inside a quadrilateral
(c) A pentagon inside a square
(d) A heptagon inside a hexagon

8. Which tangram consists of the largest number of triangles? (tangram is a puzzle consisting of seven shapes which are put together to form a shape.)

(a) 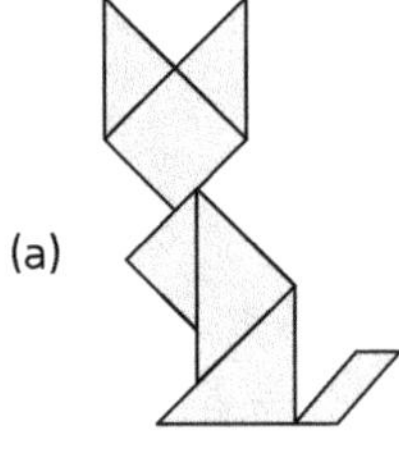   (b) 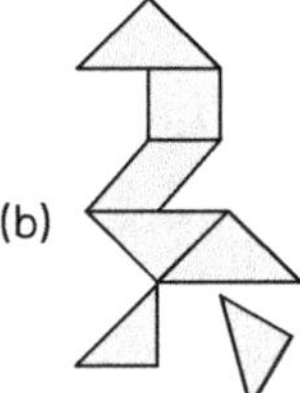

(c) 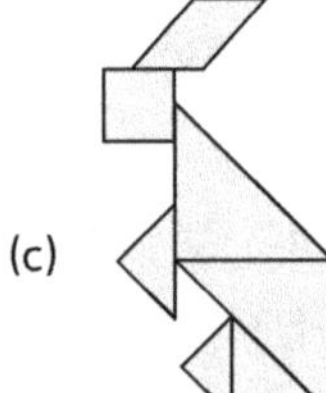   (d) All have equal number of triangles

Mathematics Olympiad Class IV

9. Which shape is represented by the given objects?

(a) Circle   (b) Cube
(c) Cylinder   (d) Cone

10. How many capital alphabets are there which have curved lines?

(a) 10   (b) 11   (c) 4   (d) 8

11. The number of edges in the adjacent figure is equal to

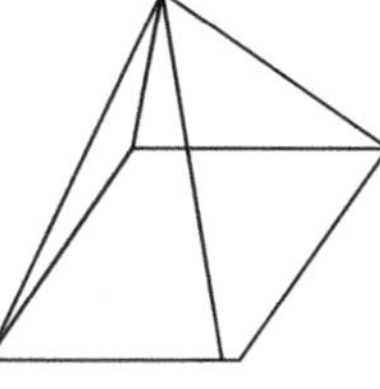

(a) 4   (b) 6   (c) 7   (d) 8

12. In the given figure, if all the points are joined, then how many line segments will you get?

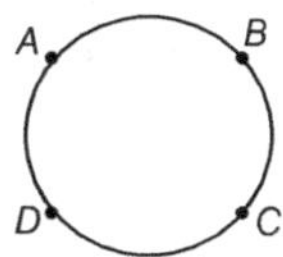

(a) 6   (b) 8
(c) 14   (d) 10

13. For an art project Simon cut a piece of paper into a shape with 4 sides, but none of them were of the same length. What is the shape of the paper?

(a) Rectangle   (b) Square
(c) Pentagon   (d) Quadrilateral

14. Following are the steps to find the centre of the circle. Arrange the steps in the correct order and choose the correct option.

  A. Fold the circle into half.

  B. The point where two creased lines intersects is the centre.

  C. Draw the circle using any circular shape.

  D. Fold the circle into another half.

(a) B C D A   (b) C A D B
(c) C D A B   (d) B C D A

15. Fill in the blanks and choose the correct option.

(i) Obtuse	(ii) Chord
(iii) Radius	(iv) Two
(v) One	(vi) Ray
(vii) Diameter	(viii) Acute

  I. Only _____ line can pass through two distinct points in a plane.

  II. _____ is twice the radius of the circle.

  III. An angle less than 90° is an _____ angle.

  IV. A _____ is a line segment that connects any two points on the circle.

	I	II	III	IV
(a)	(iv)	(ii)	(i)	(ii)
(b)	(v)	(vii)	(viii)	(ii)
(c)	(v)	(ii)	(vi)	(iii)
(d)	(iv)	(ii)	(viii)	(vii)

16. If PQ and PR are two radii of the circle, then which of the following is false?

(a) PQ and PR are equal in length
(b) PQ is also a chord of the circle
(c) P is the centre of the circle
(d) Q and R are the points on the circle

17. Louis drew a shape which consists of five angles. Which shape has been drawn by Louis?

(a) Triangle   (b) Rectangle
(c) Pentagon   (d) Hexagon

18. State true or false and choose the correct option.

  I. It is possible for two lines to intersect at two points.

  II. A circle has atmost one centre.

  III. A cuboid is a six faced figure whose each face is a rectangle.

  IV. In a $\triangle PQR$, A is a vertex.

	I	II	III	IV		I	II	III	IV
(a)	F	T	T	F	(b)	T	T	T	F
(c)	F	T	F	T	(d)	T	F	T	F

19. Which of the following angles does the given figure contain?

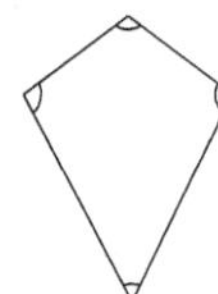

(a) Acute angle   (b) Obtuse angle
(c) Right angle   (d) All of these

20. Match the shapes with their nets and choose the correct option.

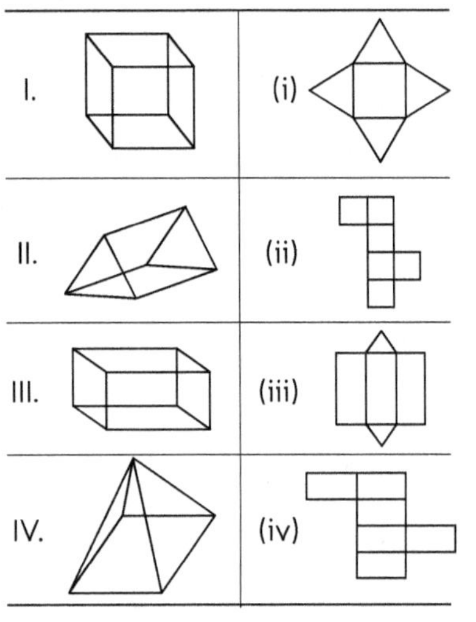

	I	II	III	IV		I	II	III	IV
(a)	(iii)	(iv)	(i)	(ii)	(b)	(ii)	(iii)	(iv)	(i)
(c)	(iv)	(iii)	(i)	(ii)	(d)	(ii)	(i)	(iv)	(iii)

21. Which of the following consists of exactly 6 faces?

(a) 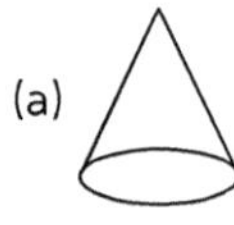   (b) 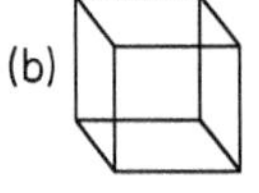

(c) 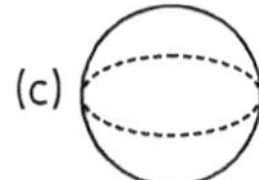   (d) 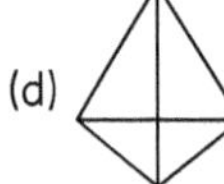

22. Which option shows three shapes that can make a rectangle when they are all joined together?

(a) 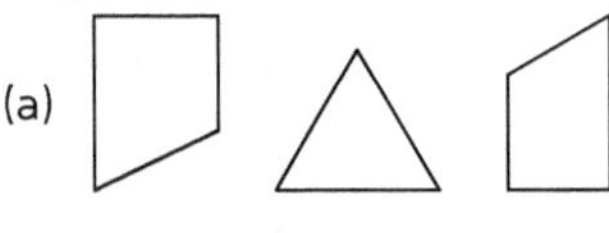

(b) 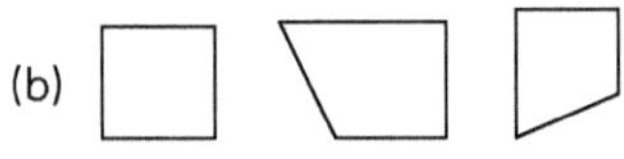

(c) 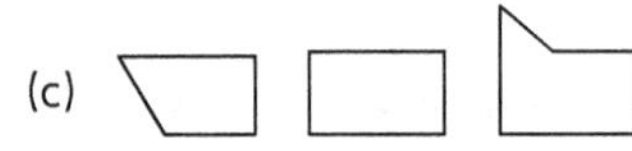

(d) 

23. Match the following and choose the correct option.

I.	I am a four sided figure. My edges are straight and I am not a square.	(i) 
II.	I have one curved surface, one flat surface, one edge and one vertex.	(ii) 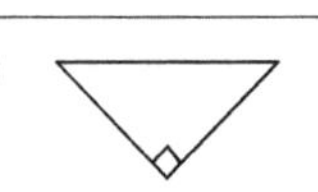
III.	I am a shape with no corners, no edges and one curved surface.	(iii)
IV.	I have three corners and one right angle. My sides need not have the same length.	(iv)

	I	II	III	IV
(a)	(ii)	(iv)	(i)	(iii)
(b)	(iv)	(iii)	(i)	(ii)
(c)	(ii)	(iii)	(iv)	(i)
(d)	(iii)	(i)	(iv)	(ii)

Mathematics Olympiad Class IV

Area and Perimeter

Perimeter It is the distance around the boundary of a shape. It is calculated by adding the lengths of all the sides of a figure.

Area The area of a figure is the number of square units that cover the surface of the closed figure.

The given chart represents the perimeter and area of some figures :

Figure	Perimeter	Area
Rectangle — Length, Breadth	2 (Length + Breadth)	Length × Breadth
Square — Side	4 × Side	Side × Side
Triangle — b, a, c	$a + b + c$	—

e.g. 1. Perimeter of a square having side 4 cm is $4 \times 4 = 16$ cm.

   2. Area of a rectangle having length 8 cm and breadth 6 cm is $8 \times 6 = 48$ sq cm.

1. What is the perimeter of the given triangle?

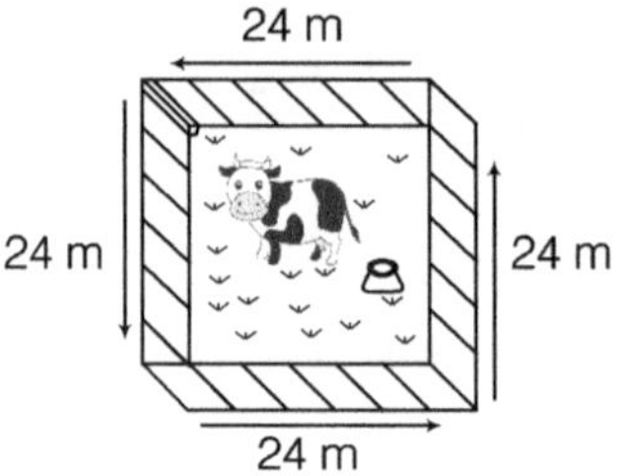

(a) 14.2 cm
(b) 16.8 cm
(c) 15.8 cm
(d) 16.2 cm

2. State true or false and choose the correct option.

   I. Area is expressed in cm^2.

   II. The measuring unit for area and perimeter is always same.

   III. Triangle is a quadrilateral.

   IV. If the side of a square park is 12 m, then its perimeter is 48 m.

	I	II	III	IV		I	II	III	IV
(a)	T	F	T	F	(b)	F	F	F	T
(c)	T	T	F	T	(d)	F	T	T	F

3. Fill in the blanks and choose the correct option.

(i) Area		(ii) $2\,abc$	
(iii) $5 \times$ sides		(iv) $a + b + c$	
(v) 15		(vi) Perimeter	
(vii) 30		(viii) $6 \times$ sides	

   I. ____ is expressed in the units of length.

   II. Perimeter of a triangle with sides a, b and c is _____ .

   III. Perimeter of a regular hexagon is _____ .

   IV. Area of 15 unit squares is ____ square units.

	I	II	III	IV
(a)	(vi)	(iii)	(viii)	(vii)
(b)	(i)	(ii)	(iii)	(v)
(c)	(vi)	(iv)	(viii)	(v)
(d)	(i)	(viii)	(iii)	(vii)

4. The cow is grazing in a field given below. Then, the area in which it can graze is

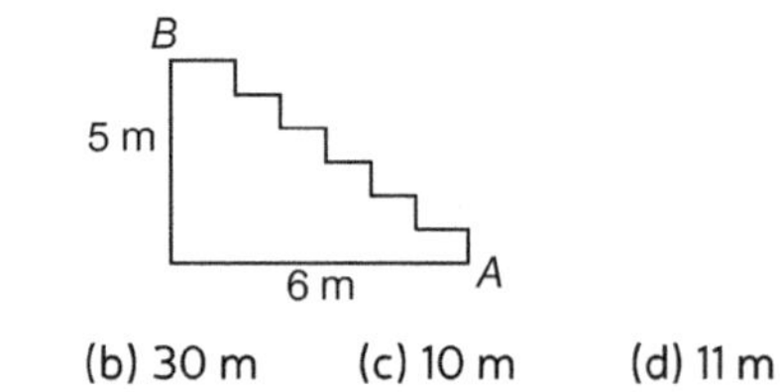

(a) 576 m²   (b) 286 m²
(c) 48 m²   (d) 76 m²

5. An ant is crawling from point *A* to point *B* using the staircase. How many metre distance will it crawl to reach point *B*?

(a) 12 m   (b) 30 m   (c) 10 m   (d) 11 m

6. Raven and Rosy took part in a race. The racing track is circular in shape. Raven runs faster than Rosy, yet she loses the race. The reason for this is

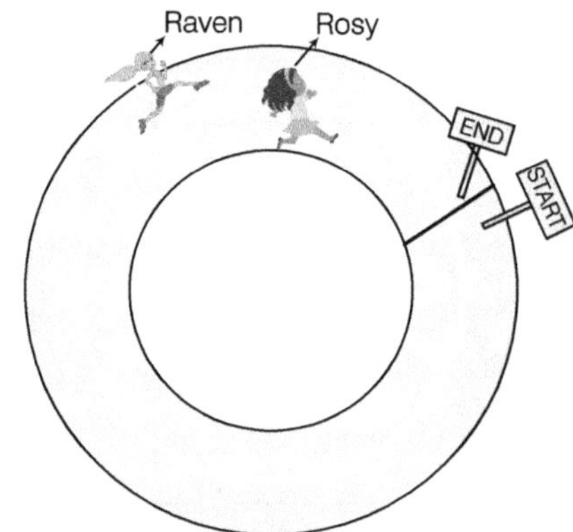

(a) The perimeter of inner circle is less than the perimeter of outer circle
(b) The area of inner circle is less than the area of outer circle
(c) Both the girls have different start and finish line
(d) Cannot be determined

7. Gregor has a piece of bread. He divided it into four pieces. If dimension of the bread is given, then the area of each piece is

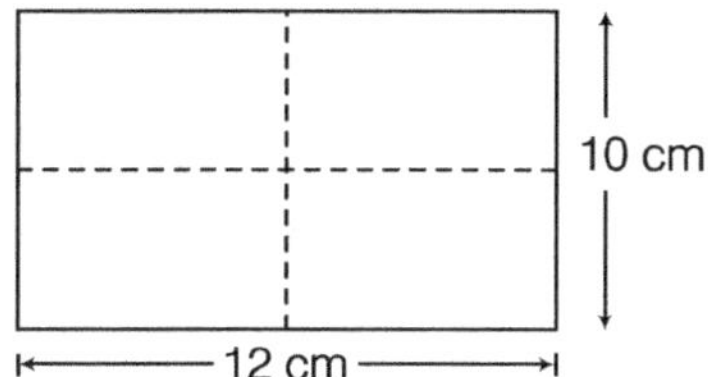

(a) 11 cm^2 (b) 120 cm^2
(c) 30 cm^2 (d) 22 cm^2

8.

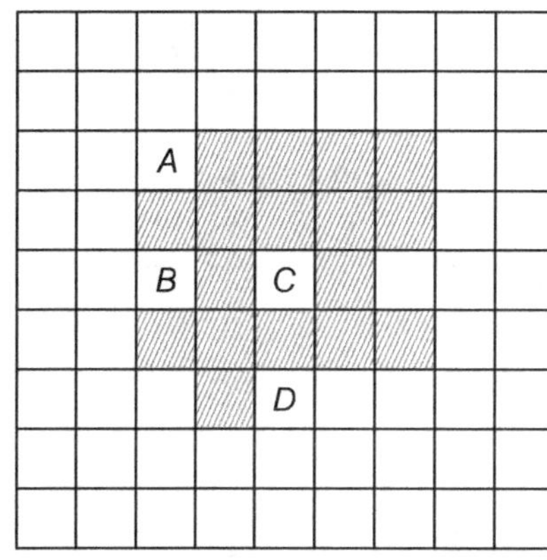

Celestia had some squares of area 1 sq unit by which she made the above figure. She is left with 1 square.

Where should the square be placed, so that the perimeter of the given figure gets reduced by 4 units?

(a) At A   (b) At B   (c) At C   (d) At D

9. Which of the following is correct?

(a) When a unit square is removed from a given shape, then both its area and perimeter get reduced by square unit and a unit respectively

(b) When a unit square is removed from a given shape, then its area gets reduced by a square unit but its perimeter either remains same or gets increased by few units

(c) When a unit square is removed from a given shape, then its area gets increased by few units but its perimeter remains same

(d) None of the above

10. Cyra is given a homework to cut-out a piece of rectangle out of a given sheet. If the breadth of the cut-out figure is 1/3rd of the breadth of the sheet as shown in the diagram, then the perimeter of the cut-out figure will be

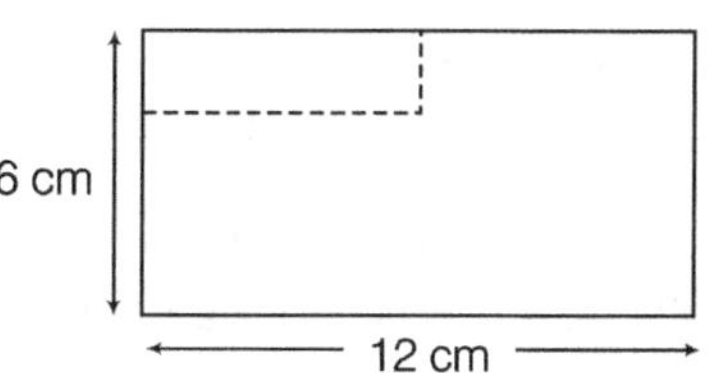

(a) 12 m   (b) 24 m   (c) 16 m   (d) 36 m

11. The given diagram shows the racing track. If a biker starts from the starting point and finishes the race first, then the total distance covered by him will be

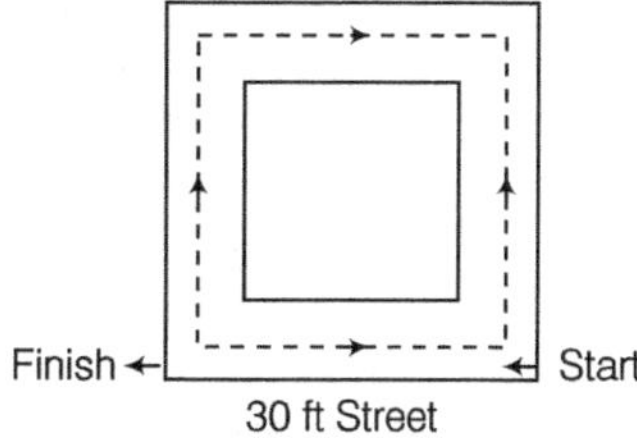

(a) 120 ft   (b) 30 ft   (c) 150 ft   (d) 100 ft

Direction (Q. Nos. 12-13) The given table shows the dimension of gardens in an apartment.

Garden	Length (in m)	Breadth (in m)
A	12	8
B	14	12
C	10	8
D	14	5

12. Which garden has the largest boundary?

(a) A   (b) B   (c) C   (d) D

13. If the breadth of the smallest garden is increased by 4 m, then what will be the position of that garden, if we arrange them in ascending order on the basis of perimeter?

(a) First   (b) Second   (c) Third   (d) Fourth

14. If each square has area 1 sq unit, then the area of the given figure is

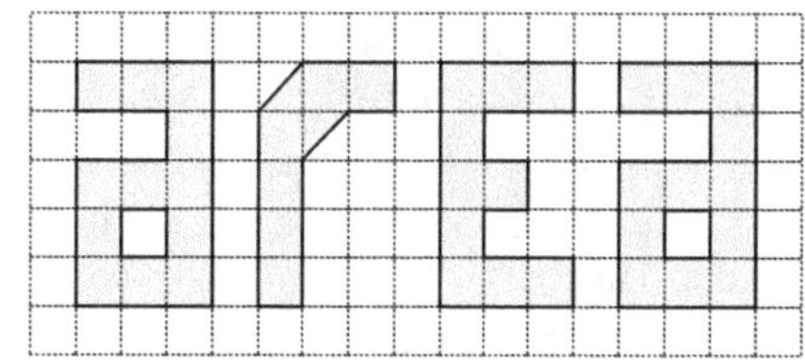

(a) 30 sq units   (b) 40 sq units
(c) 42 sq units   (d) 41 sq units

Direction (Q. Nos. 15-16) Study the following information and answer the questions.

15. If each square has area $1\,cm^2$, then which of the following given shapes occupies largest area?

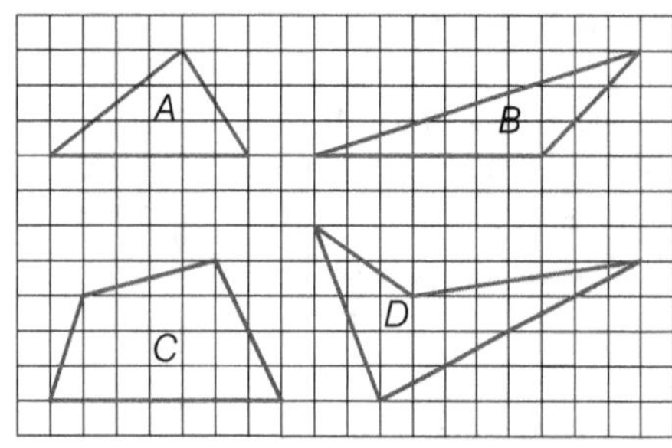

(a) A (b) B
(c) C (d) D

16. Which of the two given figures have a total area of 30 sq units (approx)?

(a) A and B
(b) B and D
(c) B and C
(d) A and C

17. A circle is inscribed in a square as shown below. Then, the area of the square is

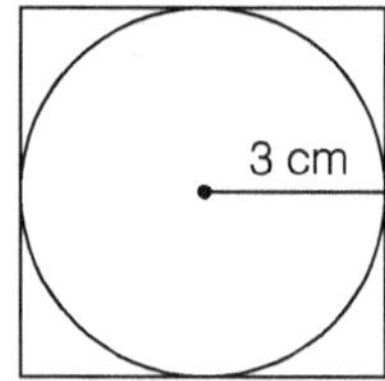

(a) $12\,cm^2$
(b) $20\,cm^2$
(c) $36\,cm^2$
(d) Cannot be determined

18. Frank's backyard is 20 sq ft and he wants the basketball court of length 5 ft and breadth 4 ft to be placed into his backyard. Does Frank have enough space?

(a) Yes, the backyard is big enough because both the backyard and basketball court are equal
(b) No, because basketball court is 24 sq ft
(c) Yes, because backyard has more area than basketball court
(d) Cannot be determined

19. Find the perimeter of the given figure and choose the correct option.

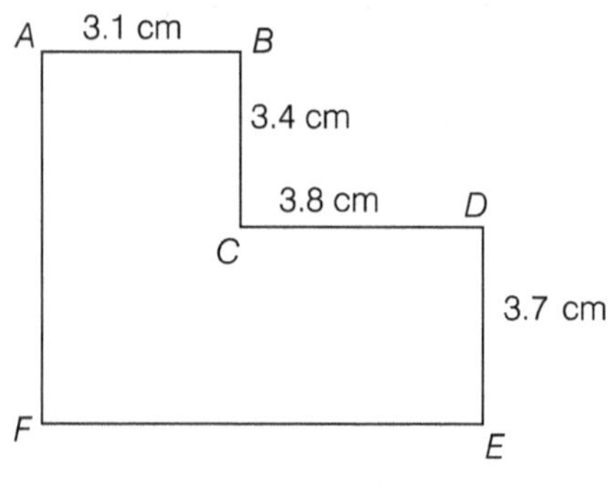

(a) 28 cm (b) 30 cm
(c) 25 cm (d) 42 cm

20. Match the following shape with their perimeter and choose the correct option.

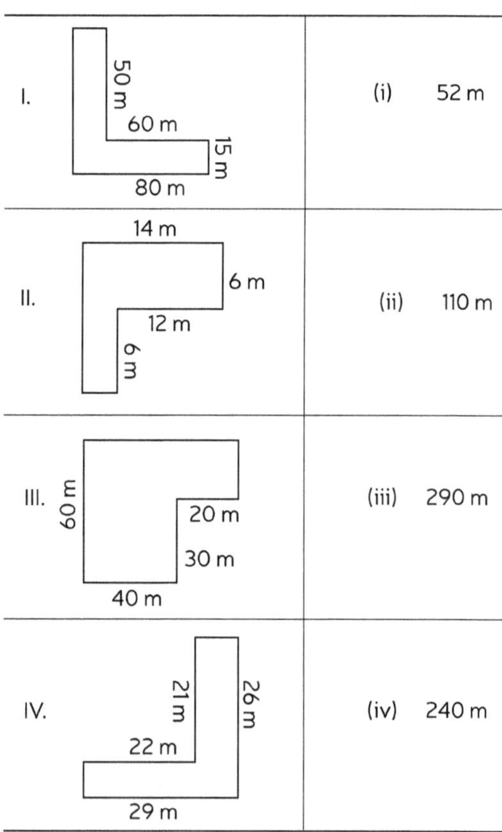

	I	II	III	IV
(a)	(iv)	(iii)	(i)	(ii)
(b)	(ii)	(iii)	(iv)	(i)
(c)	(iii)	(i)	(iv)	(ii)
(d)	(ii)	(iv)	(i)	(iii)

Mathematics Olympiad Class IV

21. Miss Michelle decided to paint a wall of her house whose length is 28 m and breadth is 21 m. If she painted one-third of the wall green and half of the remaining wall blue, then how much portion she still needs to paint?

(a) 98 m^2
(b) 392 m^2
(c) 294 m^2
(d) 196 m^2

22. Figures (i) and (ii) show two identical rectangles A and B which are arranged differently. What is the difference in the perimeter of the figures (i) and (ii)?

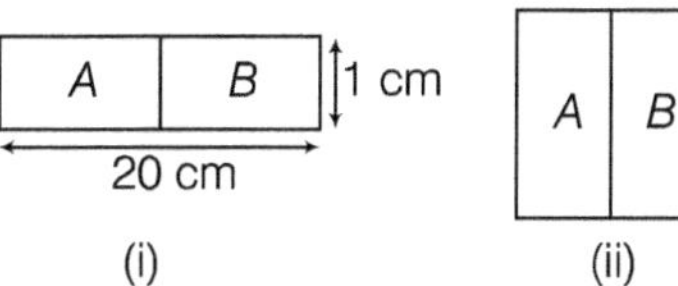

(a) 2 cm
(b) 4 cm
(c) 6 cm
(d) Both have same perimeter

23. Some girls play in a park whose dimensions are given. One day, two of them had a fight with the rest of the girls and then they decided to separate the area where they can play. They shared the area of park equally among them. How much area will be occupied by the remaining girls?

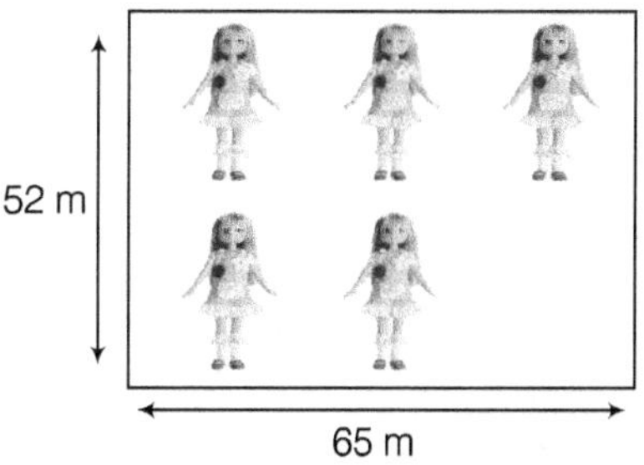

(a) 1685 m^2
(b) 2704 m^2
(c) 1352 m^2
(d) 2028 m^2

24. The perimeters of two squares are 40 cm and 32 cm. If the perimeter of the third square is equal to the difference of the perimeters of first two squares, then what will be the area of the third square?

(a) 2 cm^2 (b) 4 cm^2 (c) 64 cm^2 (d) 8 cm^2

25. The diagram shown here is the flag of Finland. Federeca is given a task of calculating the area of the flag excluding blue part. What will be the required area?

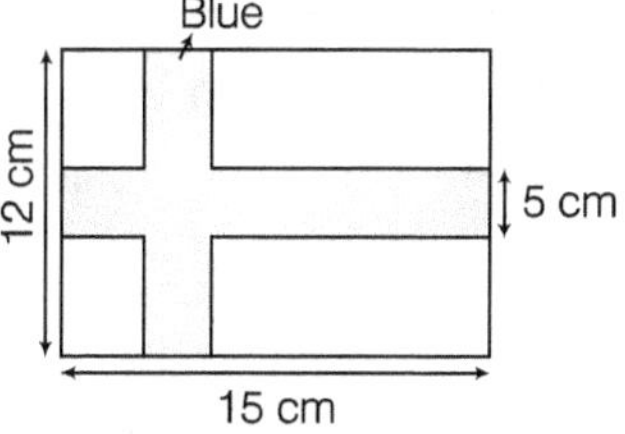

(a) 45 cm^2 (b) 70 cm^2 (c) 50 cm^2 (d) 60 cm^2

10

Pattern

This chapter consists of questions in which letters, numbers or objects are given. The student is required to study the pattern followed by the series and either complete the given series with the most suitable alternative or to find the wrong term in the series.

Example 1   Identify the pattern and find the missing term.

$$2, 4, 6, 8, ?, ?$$

Sol.   Here, the pattern is

$$2 + 2 = 4$$
$$4 + 2 = 6$$
$$6 + 2 = 8$$
$$8 + 2 = \boxed{10}$$
$$10 + 2 = \boxed{12}$$

So, the missing terms are 10 and 12.

Example 2 | A | C | | D | F | | G | I | | ? | ? |

Sol.

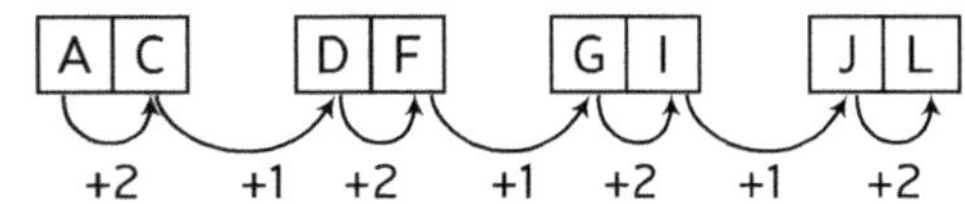

Example 3   ↑↓↑↓↑↓ ? ?

Sol.   Here, the arrow is pointing upwards and then downwards. So the next term will be ↑, ↓.

Let's Practice

1. Find the next term in the given pattern.

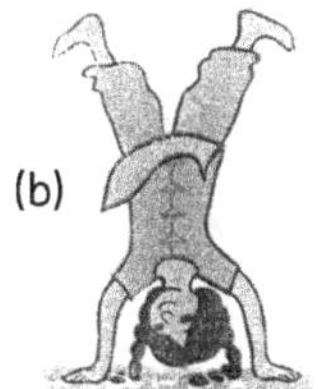

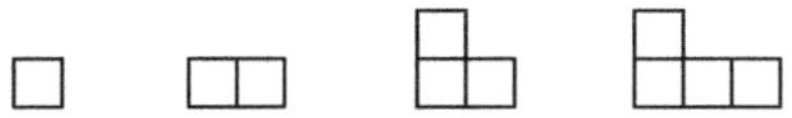

□	⊡	⊞	⊞	?
1	2	3	4	5

(a) 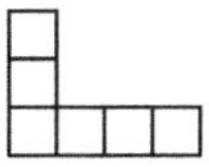 ⌐□□□ (b) 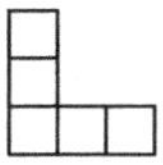 ⌐□

(c) 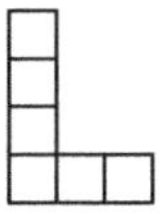 ⌐□ (d) 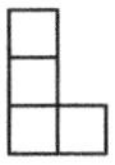 ⌐□

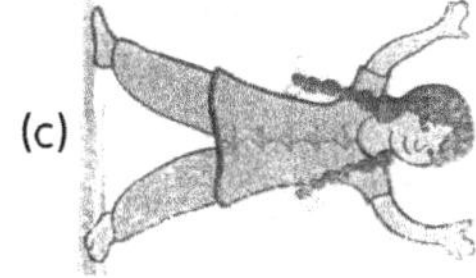

(a) [figure] (b) [figure]

(c) [figure] (d) Cannot be determined

2. The first 8 shapes of a pattern are shown below.

E ɯ Ǝ m E ɯ Ǝ m

What will be the next shape?

(a) W (b)  Ǝ

(c)  E (d) m

3. The next two shapes in the pattern given below will be

◯ □ ☆ ⬡ ◯ □ ☆ ⬡

(a)  ⬡ ◯ (b)  □ ☆

(c)  ☆ ⬡ (d)  ◯ □

4. Cyra is playing. She is showing her friends that she can stand on her head. If she continue this play, i.e. stands up and then upside down. What will be her position in 13th turn?

5. Study the pattern below and find the next two terms.

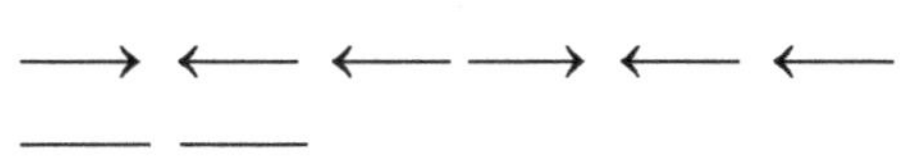

→ ← ← → ← ← ___ ___

(a) → →
(b) → →
(c) → ←
(d) ← ←

6. Observe the pattern in Ist and IIIrd row and use it to find the value of *A*.

9	4	36
5	A	60
12	7	84

(a) 12 (b) 6
(c) 11 (d) 10

Direction (Q. Nos. 7-10) Each question follows a certain pattern. Identify the pattern and choose the odd one out.

7. (a) 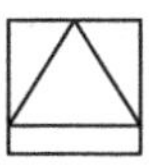 [figure] (b) [figure] (c) [figure] (d) [figure]

8. (a) Ⓔ Ⓘ (b)  Ⓐ Ⓞ

(c) 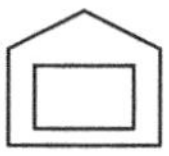 Ⓞ Ⓤ (d) Ⓕ Ⓔ

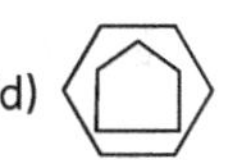

9. (a) PATTERN   (b) OLYMPIAD
   (c) MATHS   (d) RHYTHM

10.

(a) 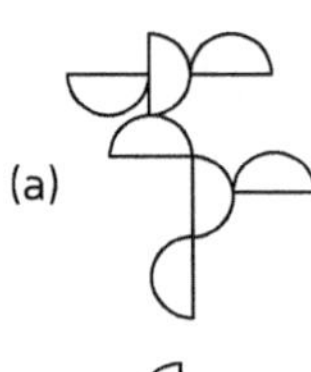   (b) 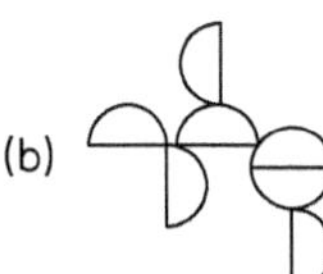

(c) 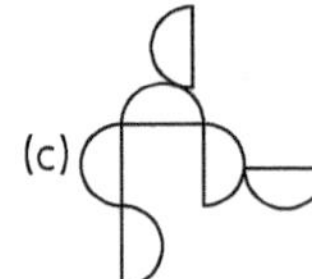   (d) 

11. Study the pattern and find the missing term.

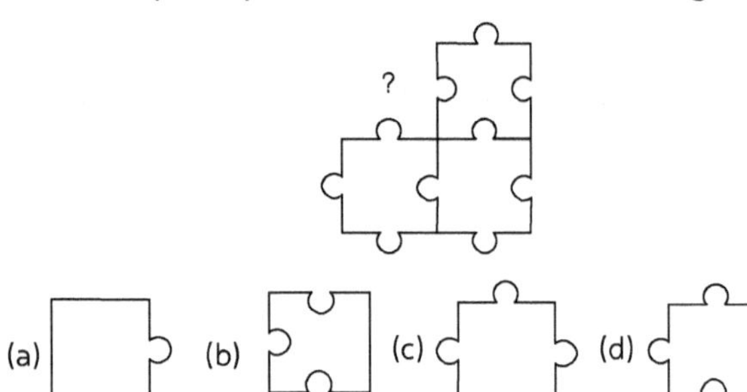

(a)      (b)      (c)      (d)

12. Identify the pattern and find the difference between *A* and *B*.

(39) (52) (65) (A) (91) (B)

(a) 26   (b) 40   (c) 58   (d) 78

13.

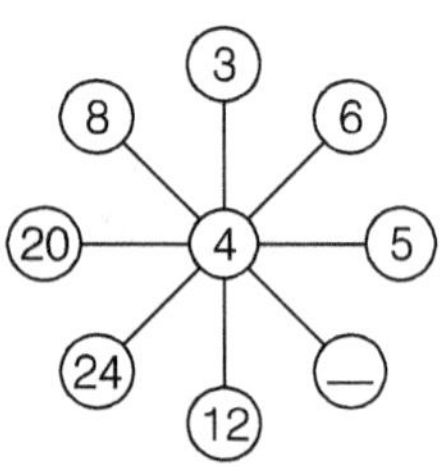

Observe the pattern and fill the missing number with correct option.

(a) 10   (b) 32   (c) 18   (d) 22

14. Fill in the blanks and choose the correct option.

(i) Bcb	(ii) cAd
(iii) Acb	(iv) cAC
(v) CDb	(vi) cdB
(vii) cbc	(viii) aDd

    I. aAbBc_d_aA_B

   II. abcaab_aabbcaab_c_

  III. abcdAbcdAB_d_BC_

  IV. aaBBc_A_bbC_

	I	II	III	IV		I	II	III	IV
(a)	(ii)	(vii)	(i)	(v)	(b)	(v)	(i)	(iii)	(viii)
(c)	(v)	(vii)	(ii)	(iv)	(d)	(i)	(vi)	(viii)	(ii)

15. Identify the pattern in the sequence

0, 1, 1, 2, 3, 5, 8, 13, ...

(a) Add 1 to the previous term to get the next term
(b) Add 2 to the previous term to get the next term
(c) Add the previous terms to get the next term
(d) Multiply the previous terms to get the next term

16.

If the above pattern continues in the same way, till 20th term, then how many times △ will occur in the pattern?

(a) 4   (b) 6
(c) 7   (d) 3

17. Match the following and choose the correct option.

I.	2	3	5	7	(i)	9	11	
II.	1	3	5	7	(ii)	22	32	
III.	3	5	8	10	(iii)	11	13	
IV.	2	4	8	14	(iv)	13	15	

Codes

	I	II	III	IV		I	II	III	IV
(a)	(i)	(iii)	(iii)	(iv)	(b)	(iv)	(i)	(ii)	(iii)
(c)	(i)	(iii)	(iv)	(ii)	(d)	(iii)	(i)	(iv)	(ii)

18. Lenore has made a pattern of numbers. She wants to check whether there is any wrong term in the pattern or not. Choose the wrong number in pattern.

10000	9200	8400	7600

(a) 10000   (b) 7600

(c) 8400   (d) All are correct

19. Following figure shows the magic pattern in which every row, column and diagonal follow certain pattern. Identify the pattern and complete it.

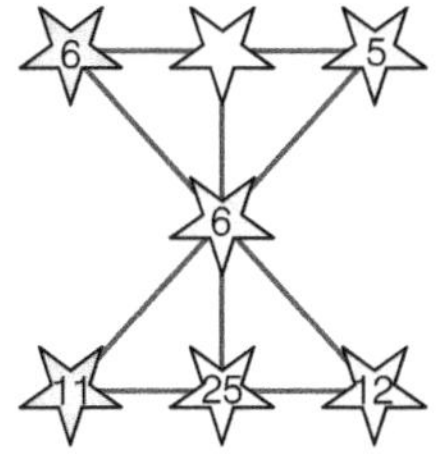

(a) 24   (b) 12   (c) 4   (d) 19

20. Find the wrong term in the pattern given below.

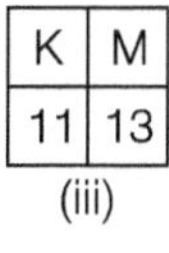

(a) (i)   (b) (iii)   (c) (ii)   (d) (iv)

21. State true or false and choose the correct option.

First six shapes of a pattern is given. If the pattern repeats itself in the same sequence as given above, then state whether the following statements are true or false.

I. The 54th shape in the sequence will be

II. If the pattern ends at the 15th step, then 7th shape from the last will be

III. If  is removed from the above pattern, then 13th shape will be

IV. The pattern with 27 steps will end with

	I	II	III	IV		I	II	III	IV
(a)	T	F	F	T	(b)	T	T	F	F
(c)	T	F	T	F	(d)	F	T	T	T

22. Choose the correct option for the given pattern.

(a) ABCCABCC
(b) ABBCDAAD
(c) ABCCBAAA
(d) ABCABCAB

Direction (Q. Nos. 23-24) Replace the question mark (?) with the correct image.

23.

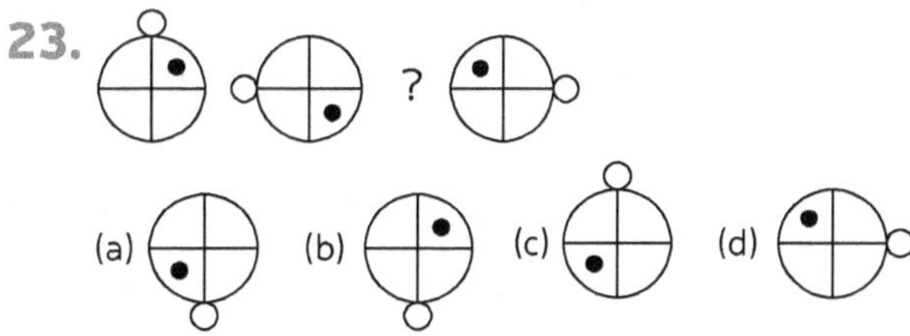

24.

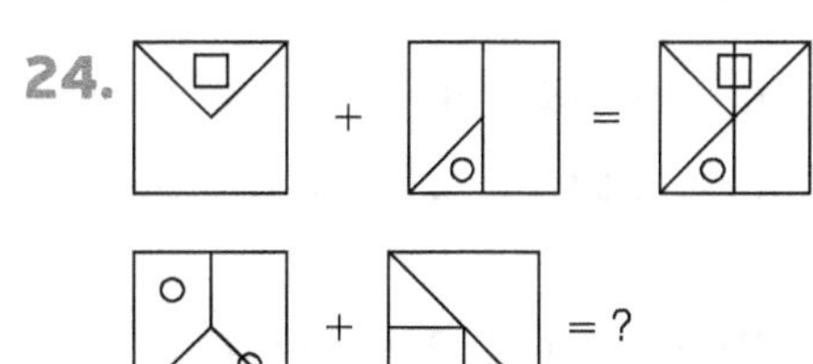

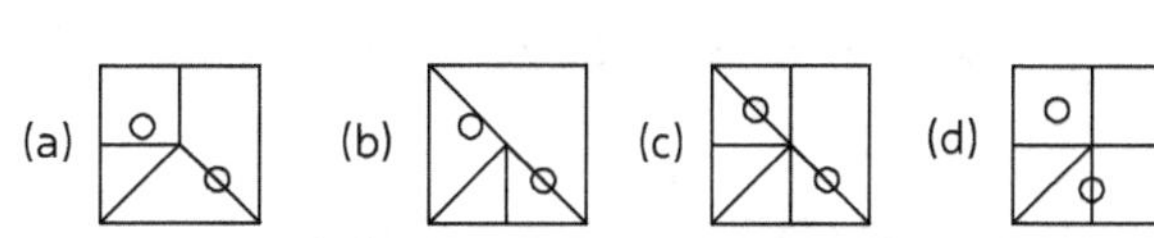

25. Verena has just started to walk. Everyday she takes two steps more than she did the day before. On the first day, she takes 2 steps and falls down. Next day, she takes 4 steps and on the third day, she takes 6 steps. How many steps will Verena be able to walk on 17th day, if she continues this pattern?

(a) 34   (b) 24
(c) 36   (d) 18

Data Handling

Collection of information is called data.

Data handling It is a process of collection, organization and representation of data in various form.

Some of the ways in which data can be represented are

- ✦ Pictograph
- ✦ Tally chart
- ✦ Tally marks
- ✦ Bar graph
- ✦ Pie chart

Pictograph   A pictograph uses pictures or symbols to show the value of the data.

Tally chart   Tally chart is a way of showing data in the form of a table by using tally marks.

Tally marks   Tally marks are a quick way of keeping track of numbers in groups of five. One vertical line is made for each of the first four numbers and the fifth number is represented by a diagonal line across the previous four.

    e.g.   卌 = 5

Bar graph   A bar graph is a graph that uses horizontal or vertical bars to display data in order to compare different quantities.

Pie chart   A pie chart is a circular chart which is divided into sectors.

    e.g.   Given pie chart shows the after-school activities of 24 children.

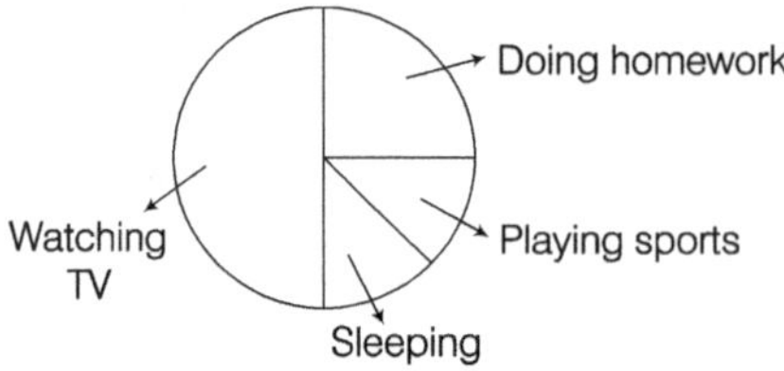

Let's Practice

1. The weights of 10 girls of class IV are 28, 25, 20, 22, 19, 26, 30, 32, 22, 21.

   What is the weight of the heaviest girl?
   (a) 34   (b) 30
   (c) 26   (d) 32

2. The pictograph shows how much a family spends on different things every month.

Rent	☐ ☐
Food	☐ ☐ ☐ ☐
Transport	☐
Others	☐ ☐ ☐

   Here, ☐ = ₹ 1000
   What does the family spend the most on?
   (a) Rent   (b) Food
   (c) Transport   (d) Others

3. A school had organised a quiz competition in which there were four teams who took part. A total of 10 questions were asked from them.

   The following table shows the number of points scored by each team.

Teams	Red	Blue	Green	Yellow
Points	7	9	10	8

   Which team scored second position in the quiz competition?
   (a) Red   (b) Blue
   (c) Green   (d) Yellow

4. The given chart shows the number of children of class IV which have their birthdays in the given three months.

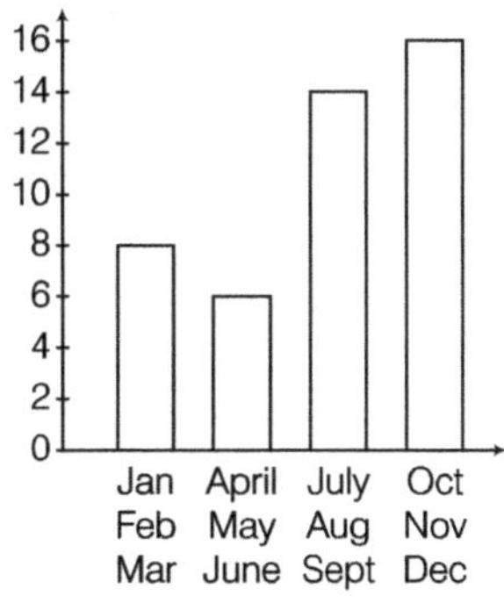

   If no children have birthday in July and only 4 children have birthday in August, then how many children have their birthdays in September?
   (a) 14   (b) 12
   (c) 10   (d) 16

5. The following pictogram shows the sale of books of a store in four different months. Then, the total sale of books in four months is

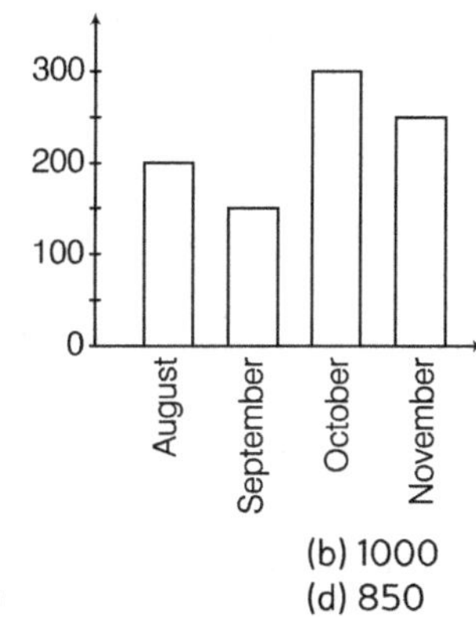

   (a) 750   (b) 1000
   (c) 900   (d) 850

6. Four children made a graph of their height.

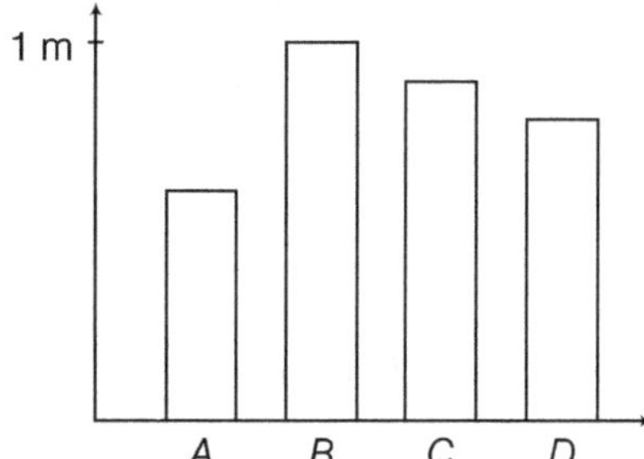

   If the comparison of the heights of the four children is as follow

        Anne > Jenny > Karen > Jai,

   then labelling of the bars of the graph would be

	A	B	C	D
(a)	Jenny	Karen	Anne	Jai
(b)	Karen	Anne	Jenny	Jai
(c)	Jai	Anne	Jenny	Karen
(d)	Anne	Karen	Jai	Jenny

7. The D' lites fast food shop wants to find out the likings of their customers whether they like burger, fries or cold coffee more. They come up with the following chart.

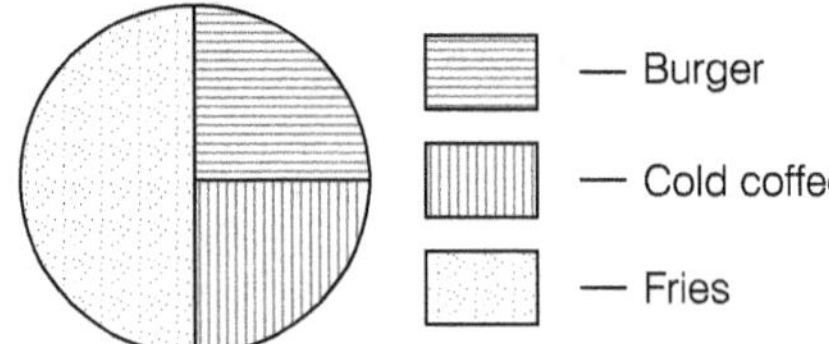

— Burger

— Cold coffee

— Fries

Which of the following is true?
(a) About one-fourth of the customers like fries
(b) About one-fourth of the customers like burger
(c) About three-fourth of the customers like cold coffee
(d) No customer likes burger

8. State true or false and choose the correct option.

   I. Data is a collection of facts such as numbers, words, measurements, observations or even just descriptions of things.

  II. When data is represented in a circle, it is called pie-chart.

 III. If four students have a score of 80 in Mathematics, then the score of 80 is said to have the frequency of 4.

 IV. In the bar graph, the data is represented using pictures.

	I	II	III	IV		I	II	III	IV
(a)	T	F	F	T	(b)	T	T	T	F
(c)	T	F	T	F	(d)	F	T	F	T

9. Class IV consists of 28 children. All children of the class are getting ready for a drama. Some children are acting, some are busy in collecting dresses while some are bringing chairs and tables to make the sets.

Work	Number of children
Acting	14
Collecting dresses	7
Making sets	7

Which of the following pie chart would be most appropriate to depict the above information?

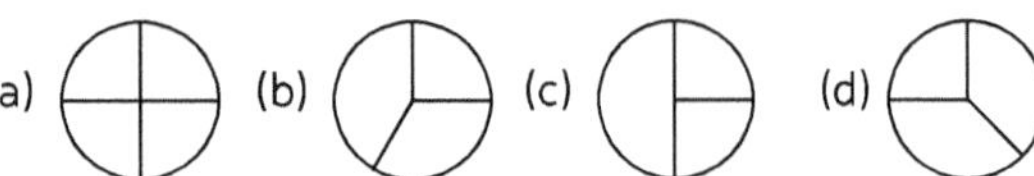

(a)   (b)   (c)   (d)

10. Krista is keeping a record of the marks she got during her class tests.

Date	1st June	3rd June	7th June	12th June	17th June
Marks (Out of 20)	15	14	10	19	13

Which of the following is true?
(a) Performance of Krista is improving each day
(b) Performance of Krista is declining each day
(c) Performance of Krista cannot be determined
(d) None of the above

11. The amount of time (in hours) that Anna practised the piano each day for 11 days is shown below.

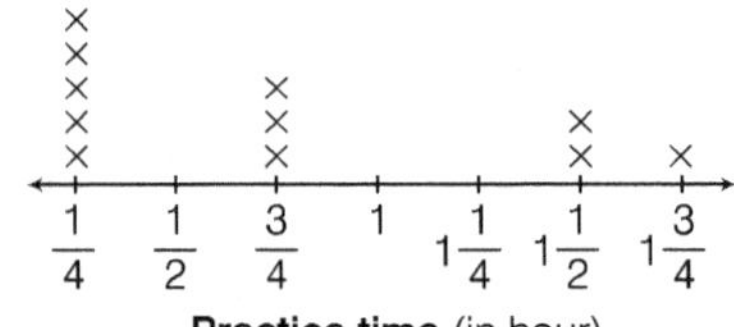

Practice time (in hour)

How many hours in total did Anna practice the piano over the 11 days?

(a) $4\dfrac{1}{4}$ (b) $6\dfrac{3}{4}$ (c) $7\dfrac{3}{4}$ (d) $8\dfrac{1}{4}$

Direction (Q. Nos. 12-13) The following pictogram shows the number of ice-creams sold within 4 days in an ice-cream parlour. Study it and answer the questions.

Day	Number of ice-creams sold
1st	
2nd	
3rd	
4th	

Given, = 4 ice-creams

and = 2 ice-creams

12. On which day, 14 ice-creams were sold?
(a) 1st   (b) 2nd   (c) 3rd   (d) 4th

13. On which two days, a total of 36 ice-creams were sold?
(a) 2 and 4   (b) 1 and 3   (c) 3 and 4   (d) 1 and 2

14. The following list shows the number of cars sold in a company on particular days.

Day	Number of cars
A-Monday	‖‖ ‖‖
B-Tuesday	‖‖ ‖‖‖‖
C-Wednesday	‖‖
D-Thursday	‖‖
E-Friday	‖‖ ‖

‖‖ represents → 5 cars

Arrange the days in ascending order on the basis of number of cars sold each day.

(a) $C < D < A < B < E$
(b) $A < B < D < E < C$
(c) $B < A < E < D < C$
(d) $C < D < E < A < B$

Direction (Q. Nos. 15-16) Venkateshwara Global school conducted a survey of class IV to identify the interest of students in different Olympiads. The data is as follows

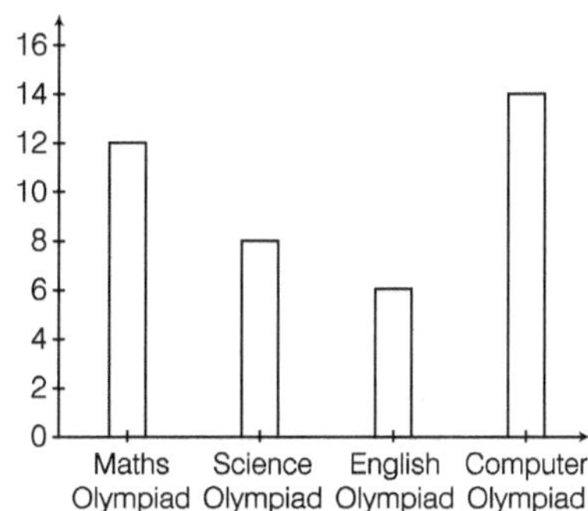

15. In which Olympiad, students are interested the most?

(a) Maths
(b) Science
(c) English
(d) Computer

16. How many more students are interested in Maths Olympiad than English Olympiad?

(a) 14
(b) 8
(c) 6
(d) 10

17. Eliana is very fond of collecting data. She made the following list of those houses in her colony who have a particular pet.

Pet	Dog	Cat	Rabbit	Tortoise	Parrot
Frequency	12	7	☐	1	5	30

How many houses have rabbit as their pet?

(a) 4
(b) 8
(c) 5
(d) 6

Direction (Q. Nos. 18-20) Consider the following bar graph and answer the questions.

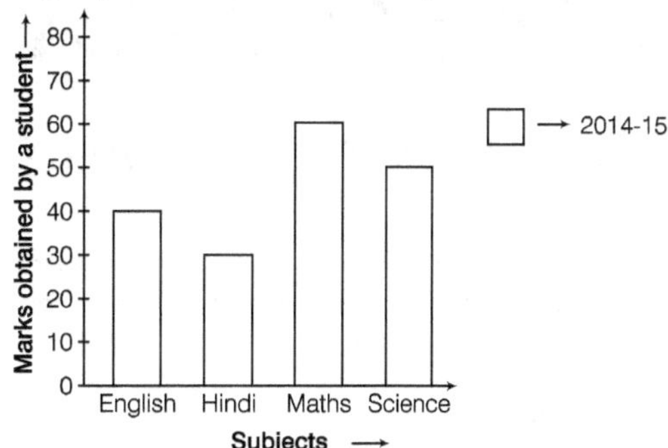

18. What is the information given by the bar graph?

(a) Marks obtained by a student in four subjects
(b) Marks obtained by a student in session 2014-15
(c) Marks obtained by a student in three subjects
(d) Both (a) and (b)

19. In which subject did the student score second highest marks?

(a) English (b) Hindi (c) Maths (d) Science

20. In which subject, did the student's score is $\frac{3}{4}$ th of the score in English?

(a) Maths
(b) Hindi
(c) Science
(d) None of these

Direction (Q. Nos. 21-22) A group of kids went on a summer camp. At the end of the week, the counselors asked campers what was their favourite part of camp. This pie-graph represents the response of kids.

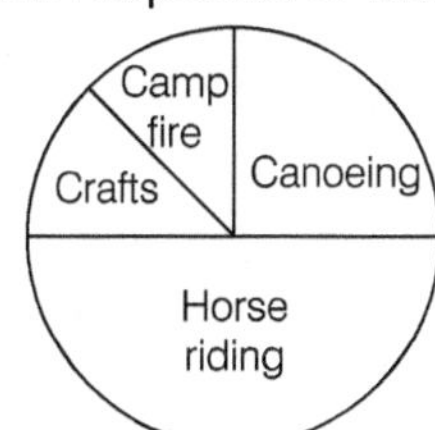

21. What fraction of campers choose canoeing as their favourite activity?

(a) $\frac{3}{4}$ (b) $\frac{1}{2}$ (c) $\frac{3}{2}$ (d) $\frac{1}{4}$

22. The fraction which represent number of children who choose crafts and horse riding as their favourite activity is

(a) $\frac{5}{8}$ (b) $\frac{2}{4}$ (c) $\frac{3}{8}$ (d) $\frac{1}{4}$

Practice Set 1

A Whole Content Based Test for Class 4th Mathematics Olympiad

1. The population of the city where Diana born is 145526. What is the population when rounded off to nearest thousand?
(a) 145000
(b) 145600
(c) 145500
(d) 146000

2. Look at the given numbers.

Which two numbers should be selected from the above box, so that the following equation becomes true?

$$\boxed{} \times \boxed{} = 342$$

(a) 18, 16
(b) 17, 19
(c) 18, 19
(d) 17, 16

3. Tancy daily studies for few hours. She studied 6 hours on Monday, as shown in the model.

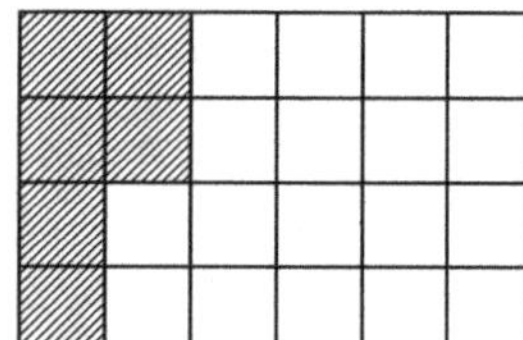

On Tuesday, she studied for more hours than on Monday. Which of the following fractions could represent the number of hours Tancy studied on Tuesday?
(a) $\dfrac{1}{6}$
(b) $\dfrac{1}{8}$
(c) $\dfrac{2}{4}$
(d) $\dfrac{24}{24}$

4. Which statement about $\dfrac{3}{4}$ and $\dfrac{9}{10}$ is true?
(a) $\dfrac{3}{4} = \dfrac{9}{10}$ because $4 - 3 = 1$ and $10 - 9 = 1$
(b) $\dfrac{3}{4} = \dfrac{9}{10}$ because $3 + 6 = 9$ and $4 + 6 = 10$
(c) $\dfrac{3}{4} < \dfrac{9}{10}$ because $3 < 9$ and $4 < 10$
(d) $\dfrac{3}{4} < \dfrac{9}{10}$ because $\dfrac{3}{4}$ is less than $\dfrac{4}{5}$ and $\dfrac{9}{10}$ is greater than $\dfrac{4}{5}$

5. Mia read 0.42 pages of a story book. How many pages Mia read, if the total number of pages is 100?
(a) 4.2
(b) 42
(c) 4
(d) 420

6. The total number of sugar packets of 300 g required to make 4.5 kg are
(a) 3
(b) 12
(c) 15
(d) 20

7. Which term means a figure that is formed by two rays or two line segments with a common end point?
(a) Vertex
(b) Angle
(c) Edge
(d) Intersecting lines

8. Gretta poured juice into a measuring container like the one shown. How much juice is in the container?

(a) $\dfrac{1}{2}$ cup
(b) $2\dfrac{1}{5}$ cup
(c) $1\dfrac{1}{2}$ cup
(d) $2\dfrac{1}{3}$ cup

9. A student is given the dimensions of rectangles A, B and C. Help him/her to find the rectangle(s) whose perimeter is greater than or equal to its area.
A : length = 8.5 cm, breadth = 2 cm
B : length = 5 cm, breadth = 4 cm
C : side = 4 cm
(a) A
(b) B
(c) Both A and C
(d) Both B and C

10. George bought 30 pencils and 20 pens for ₹ 5 and ₹ 10 each respectively. He wants to distribute it among the maximum number of children. What is the amount each child will pay to the Geroge?
(a) ₹ 50
(b) ₹ 15
(c) ₹ 35
(d) ₹ 40

11. How many letters in the English alphabet cannot be folded into halves?

(a) 10   (b) 11

(c) 12   (d) 13

Direction (Q. No. 12) *Sue ordered some pizza for her friends. She surveyed toppings that they would like on their pizzas.*

Toppings	Number of votes
Cheese	III
Pepperoni	NN I
Sausage	IIII
Mushroom	–
Onion	II

12. What can Sue most likely conclude from her survey?

(a) Most of Sue's friend like cheese than pepperoni pizza

(b) Sausage is the group's second favourite type of pizza

(c) Sue needs to order only 1 onion pizza

(d) A pizza with both pepperoni and mushroom should be ordered

13. Austen has two piggy banks. In Ist bank, she collected coins and in 2nd bank, she collected notes.

The money in each piggy bank is shown below

Piggy bank I

Piggy bank II

How much money Austen have in total when rounded off to nearest ten?

(a) ₹ 110

(b) ₹ 100

(c) ₹ 115

(d) ₹ 120

Direction (Q. Nos. 14-15) *The following graph shows the number of spectators that were present at each event of olympic games. Use the graph to answer the questions.*

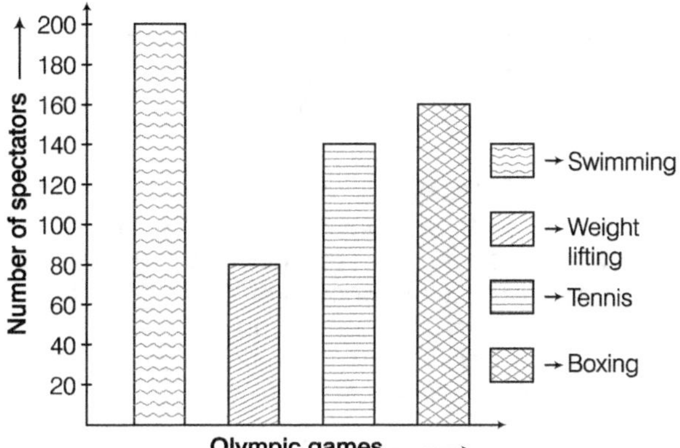

14. How many spectators were there at the boxing event?

(a) 140

(b) 130

(c) 160

(d) 180

15. The difference between the maximum and minimum number of spectators in these events is

(a) 100

(b) 80

(c) 60

(d) 120

Practice Set 2

A Whole Content Based Test for Class 4th Mathematics Olympiad

1. Louisa has some candies in her bag. She can give an equal number of pieces of candy to 5, 3 or 2 people. Which number of pieces of candy could be in Louisa's bag?
(a) 12   (b) 20
(c) 30   (d) 45

2. Adira's birthday is coming. Her mom decided to throw a birthday party. There are 18 children who will come in her birthday party and each child will require 2 scoops of ice-creams. If Adira's mom can get 6 scoops of ice-creams out of every container, then how many containers will Adira's mom require?
(a) 3   (b) 4
(c) 6   (d) 9

3. Anouk is playing ludo with four of his friends. Each player throws two dice at a time, then add the numbers on dice and move the tokens forward. What is the maximum number of squares that can be jumped by the token throwing both the dice once?

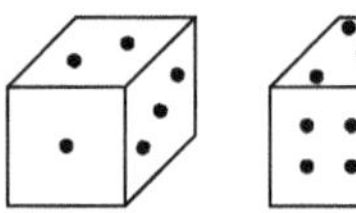

(a) 9   (b) 11
(c) 15   (d) 12

4. Here are some clues regarding a number.

   I. It is an even number.
   II. It is a multiple of 5 and factor of 10.
   III. It is less than 27.
The number that fits in all the clues is
(a) 5   (b) 10
(c) 20   (d) 25

5. Which of the given figures has maximum number of obtuse angles?

(a) 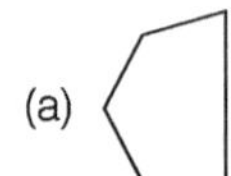 (b) 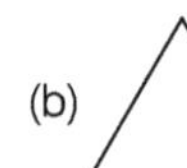 (c) ⬡ (d) ⬡

6. If the HCF of first two multiples of a number is one of numbers, then their LCM is
(a) same as HCF
(b) other number
(c) any one of the two numbers
(d) Cannot be determined

7. Daniel has a chart paper in which he puts his stamps. If the length and breadth of the chart paper is 13 cm and 8 cm respectively, then how many stamps could be placed inside the chart paper, if each stamp occupies an area of 2 cm²?
(a) 50
(b) 52
(c) 48
(d) 54

8. Decode the word after arranging the decimal in decreasing order and choose the correct option.

$$\begin{array}{cccc} 1.25 & 3.98 & 4.84 & 6.53 \\ +\,2.95 & \times\,4 & \div\,2 & -\,1.64 \\ \hline \text{M} & \text{T} & \text{E} & \text{A} \end{array}$$

(a) MEAT   (b) MATE
(c) TEAM   (d) TAME

9. Joy wrote expression below:
$$(8 \times 2) \times 5$$
Which expression is equivalent to Joy's expression?
(a) $(8 + 2) \times 5$
(b) $(8 \times 2) + 5$
(c) $8 \times (2 \times 5)$
(d) $8 \times (2 \div 5)$

10. Allen is writing a poem. He writes 7 words on the first line, 12 words on the second line, 17 words on the third line. If the pattern continues in the same way, then how many words will Allen write on the eighth line?
(a) 42
(b) 37
(c) 47
(d) 34

11. Zandra joined the dance classes. Her teacher charges ₹ 150 for every class of one hour. If Zandra joined the classes on 15th April, 2015 and continued it till 19th June, then how much money does Zandra owe to her dance teacher, assuming that there are no extra classes and a holiday on Sunday?

April 2015

S	M	T	W	T	F	S
			1	2	3	4
5	6	7	8	9	10	11
12	13	14	15	16	17	18
19	20	21	22	23	24	25
26	27	28	29	30		

(a) ₹ 9900
(b) ₹ 9000
(c) ₹ 8550
(d) ₹ 11250

12. Which number replaces the question mark?

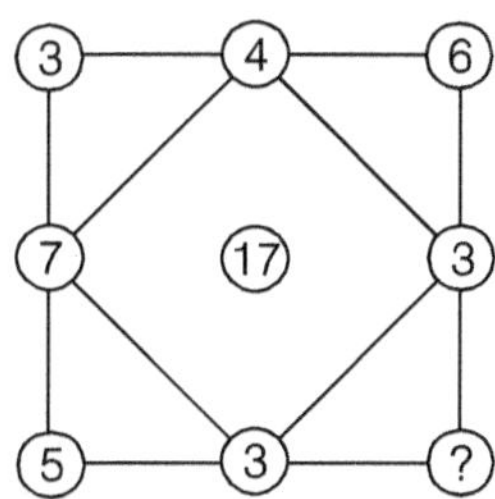

(a) 2
(b) 4
(c) 3
(d) 5

13. Eeva has climbed 15 stairs. She needs to climb a total of 25 stairs. The shaded region of which figure models the number of stairs Eeva has climbed out of the total number she needs to climb?

(a) 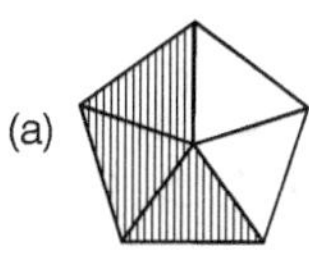 (b) 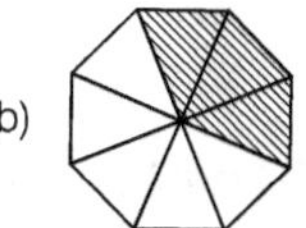

(c) 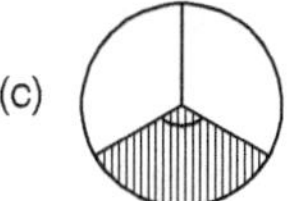 (d) 

14. How many triangles are there in the figure given below?

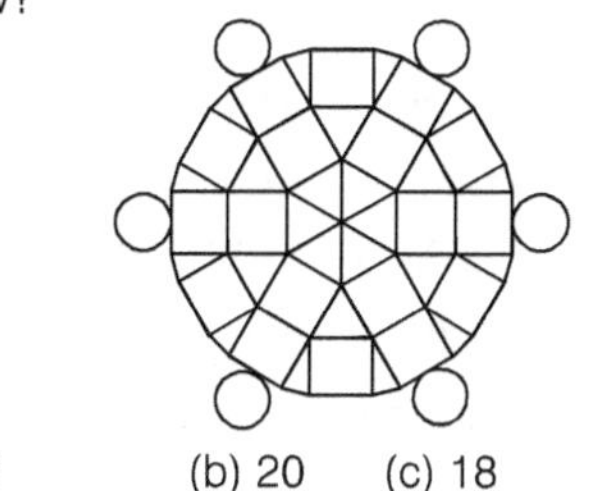

(a) 12 (b) 20 (c) 18 (d) 24

15. The graph shows the number of plants Krista and her friends planted each day in a garden.

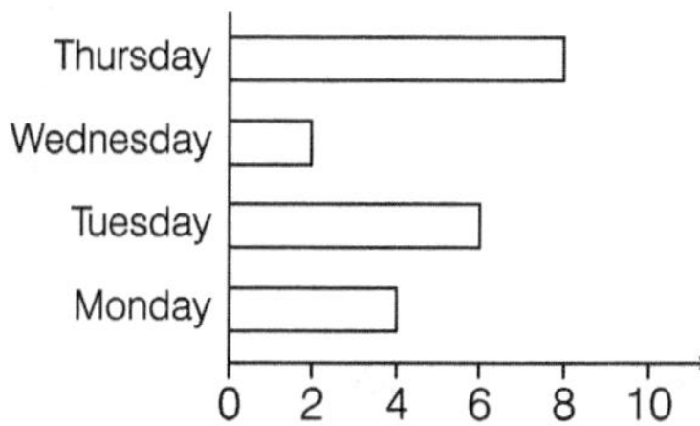

If each sapling requires 30 minutes to get planted and they started planting at 5 : 00 O'clock in the evening on Tuesday, then at what time Krista and her friends get their work done?

(a) 8:00 am (b) 8:00 pm
(c) 7:00 pm (d) 7:30 pm

Answers *and* Solutions

① Knowing Our Numbers

1. Eighty six thousand four hundred can be written
(c) as $80000 + 6000 + 400 = 86400$.

2. The sum of the given numbers
(b)
$$= 435900 + 455500 = 891400$$
Here, '4' is at hundred place, so its place value in 891400 is 400.

3. We have, $100 \text{ ones} = 100 \times 1 = 100$
(d)
$$10 \text{ tens} = 10 \times 10 = 100$$
$$1 \text{ hundred} = 1 \times 100 = 100$$
$$100 \text{ tens} = 100 \times 10 = 1000$$
So, option (d) is the odd one.

4. Observe the ones place of 295.
(a) Since, digit on the ones place $= 5$
Hence, 295 will be rounded to the next ten.
So, 295 gives 300 when rounded off to nearest ten.

5. Observe the ones and tens place of 320 which is
(a) 20.
Since, $20 < 50$
$\therefore$ 320 will be rounded to previous hundred.
Hence, 320 when rounded off to nearest hundred is 300.

6. $596280 = 500000 + 90000 + 6000 + 200 + 80$
(a)

7. Since, the ascending order of given number is
(c) $6876 < 6887 < 6909 < 6916$
So, 6876 is the least number of pages in the given table.
Hence, Sonia read the least number of pages in the month of March.

8. The pages which contain the digit '0' are 10, 20,
(b) 30, 40, 50, 60, 70, 80, 90, 100, 101, 102, 103, 104, 105, 106, 107, 108, 109, 110, 120, 130, 140, 150, 160.
So, there are 25 pages which contain the digit '0' in a book of 160 pages.

9. The number should be greater than 1898 but
(b) less than 2098.
$$1836 < 1898$$
$$1899 > 1898 \text{ and } 1899 < 2098$$

$$1888 < 1898 \text{ and } 1829 < 1898$$
So, option (b) satisfies given condition.

10. Here, the required number has 5 digits.
(b) i.e. it will be of the form

Ten th	Th	Hundred	Tens	Ones
I	II	III	IV	V

To make the smallest number using the given digits. The smallest digits will be put at the highest place and so on,.
'0' cannot be used on the ten thousand place.
Now, among 2, 3, 6, 7, we have 2 as the smallest digit. So, 2 will take the ten thousand place.

$$\frac{2}{\text{I}} \ \underline{\ } \ \underline{\ } \ \underline{\ } \ \underline{\ }$$
I II III IV V

Now, IInd place will have smallest digit among 3, 0, 6, 7. So '0' will come at IInd place.
Similarly, IIIrd digit $= 3$,
IVth digit $= 6$ and Vth digit $= 7$
$\therefore$ The number formed $= 20367$, which is odd.

11. Amount spent by three persons to buy
(c) household items $= ₹ (1072 + 260 + 128)$
$$= ₹ 1460$$
Now, $1460 = 1 \times 1000 + 4 \times 100 + 6 \times 10 + 0$
$$= 1 \text{ thousand} + 4 \text{ hundred} + 6 \text{ tens} + 0 \text{ ones}$$
Hence, there are 6 tens in the total amount spent by three persons.

12.   I. One crore is an 8-digit number, since
(b) $1 \text{ crore} = 10000000$

  II. Successor of largest 4-digit number (9999)
     $= 9999 + 1 = 10000 = $ Smallest 5-digit number

  III. 0 number has no roman numeral.

  IV. Difference between successor and predecessor of a number is always 2.

13. Place value model shows 7 hundred, 4 tens and
(d) 1 ones $= 700 + 40 + 1 = 741$

14. Checking each option carefully, we get 34 tens
(a) 47 ones $= 34 \times 10 + 47 \times 1 = 340 + 47 = 387$
(b) 42 tens 7 ones $= 42 \times 10 + 7 \times 1$
$$= 420 + 7 = 427$$

(c) 41 tens 27 ones $= 41 \times 10 + 27 \times 1$
$$= 410 + 27 = 437$$
(d) 82 tens 22 ones
$$= 82 \times 10 + 22 \times 1 = 820 + 22 = 842$$
So, option (a) does not have digit 4 in it.

15. Here,
(c)

LIV	<	XCIX
(54)		(99)
XLIV	<	XLVI
(44)		(46)
CCV	>	XCV
(205)		(95)

Hence, option (c) is correct.

16. Among the given options, only 453364 when
(c) rounded off to nearest 100 gives 453400, since $64 > 50$.

So, actual population of Bolivia is 453364.

17. V represents 5 in roman numeral.
(a)

18. Given,
(d) Number of copies sold of All sports magazine
$$= MCCCLIII$$
$$= 1000 + 100 + 100 + 100 + 50 + 3 = 1353$$
Number of copies sold of Teenage magazine
$$= MCXXIII$$
$$= 1000 + 100 + 10 + 10 + 3 = 1123$$
Number of copies sold of Young people magazine $= DXXIV = 500 + 10 + 10 + 4 = 524$
Number of copies sold of Music time magazine
$$= DCCXLVIII$$
$$= 500 + 100 + 100 + (50 - 10) + 8 = 748$$
So, Music time magazine sold 748 copies which has 4 in tens place.

19. $9243 = 9 \times 1000 + 2 \times 100 + 4 \times 10 + 3 \times 1$
(b)
$$= 9000 + 200 + 40 + 3$$
$$= 9 \text{ thousand} + 2 \text{ hundred} + 4 \text{ tens} + 3 \text{ ones}$$

20. 926543 — Successor of 926542
(a)
10000 — Smallest 5-digit number
962540 — Place value of 2 is 2000
100000 — 100039 when rounded off to nearest 100

21. Successor of $67854398 = 67854399$
(c)
Predecessor of $54677456 = 54677455$

Required difference
$$= 67854399 - 54677455 = 13176944$$
So, '2' does not appear in the required difference.

22. Possible combinations of cards
(d)
$$= 947, 974, 497, 479, 749, 794$$

23. (i) True, since in 380, we have $80 > 50$, so it
(c) will be rounded off to next nearest hundred.

(ii) False, $CCXLV = (100 + 100) + (50 - 10) + 5$
$$= 200 + 40 + 5 = 245$$

(iii) False, smallest 4-digit number that can be formed by using the digits 3, 5, 8, 0 is 3058.

(iv) True, largest 4-digit number $= 9999$
Smallest 4-digit number $= 1000$
$\therefore$ Sum $= 9999 + 1000 = 10999$

24.
(c)
$$5 \text{ tens} = 5 \times 10 = 50$$
$$8 \text{ thousand} = 8 \times 1000 = 8000$$
$$2 \text{ ones} = 2 \times 1 = 2$$
6 ten thousand $= 60000$
0 ones $= 0$
So, mystery number
$$= 60000 + 8000 + 50 + 2 = 68052$$

25. Here, $MCCLIII = 1253$
(d)
$$MMMD = 3500$$
$$MMMMDXCIV = 4594$$
$$MMCDXC = 2490$$
Option (a), $1253 < 4594$
Option (b), $3500 > 1253$
Option (c), $4594 > 2490$
Option (d), $4594 > 3500$
Hence, option (d) correctly compares the number of gallons in two of the pools.

26. Largest number formed by using the digits 5, 4,
(a) 2, 6, 0 $= 65420$

To make the largest number from the given digits, greatest digit will be put at the highest place and so on.

Smallest 5-digit number formed by using the digits 5, 4, 2, 6, 0 $= 20456$

To make the smallest number from the given digits, smallest digit will be put at the highest place and so on.

$\therefore$ Required difference $= 65420 - 20456$
$$= 44964$$

27. Smallest number $= 689$
(b) Digit at the hundred place of smallest number $= 6$
Largest number $= 986$
Digit at the hundred place of largest number $= 9$
$\therefore$ Required sum $= 9 + 6 = 15$

28. Place value of 9 in $26594325 = 90000$
(a)
$$[\because 9 \text{ is at ten thousand place}]$$
$\therefore$ Required difference $= 90000 - 9 = 89991$

29. Given, cost of book $= LXXXVI$
(b)
$$= 50 + 10 + 10 + 10 + 6 = 86$$

Cost of hockey stick $= CLV = 100 + 50 + 5 = 155$
Cost of bottle $= LXVII = 50 + 10 + 7 = 67$
Cost of paper clip $= XXV = 10 + 10 + 5 = 25$
From the above data, it is clear that hockey stick is costliest.

30. Total cost of a paper clip, hockey stick and a
(a) book $= 25 + 155 + 86$
$$= 266$$
$$= 100 + 100 + 50 + 10 + 6$$
$$= CCLXVI$$

② Operations on Numbers

1. Given, number of pennies in bag $1 = 621$
(b) Number of pennies in bag $2 = 273$
Number of pennies in bag $3 = 442$
Number of pennies in bag $4 = 385$
$\therefore$ Total number of pennies John had
$$= 621 + 273 + 442 + 385 = 1721$$
Rounded off to nearest hundred, we get
$$\text{Total} = 1700 \ (21 < 50)$$
So, 1721 will be rounded off to 1700.

Alternate Method
Rounded off to nearest hundred of all the given numbers $= 600 + 300 + 400 + 400 = 1700$

2. Given, Sum of two numbers $= 17643$
(b) One number $= 6689$
$\therefore$ Other number $= 17643 - 6689 = 10954$

3. 3×4 means, the figure having 3 rows and
(d) 4 columns.
Option (a) having 3 rows and 3 columns. In option (b) and option (c) rows and columns are not clear. Option (d) having 3 rows and 4 columns.
Hence, option (d) is the correct answer.

4. Plants planted in Delhi $= 6598$
(b) Plants planted in Uttar Pradesh $= 2593$
To find the required number of plants in Delhi than Uttar Pradesh we will find the difference between plants planted in Delhi and Uttar Pradesh
$\therefore$ Required difference $= (6598 - 2593) = 4005$
Hence, 4005 more plants are planted in Delhi.

5. Option (a), $23 \times 18 = 414$
(a) Option (b), $52 \times 22 = 1144$
Option (c), $44 \times 26 = 1144$
Option (d), $104 \times 11 = 1144$
Except 23×18, all other options have product 1144.

6. Numbers on a telephone keypad are 1, 2, 3, 4, 5,
(d) 6, 7, 8, 9, 0.
We know that, any number multiplied by 0 is 0 itself.
$\therefore$ Product of all the numbers on a telephone keypad
$$= 1 \times 2 \times 3 \times 4 \times 5 \times 6 \times 7 \times 8 \times 9 \times 0 = 0$$

7. For verification, we have the rule
(d) Dividend $=$ Divisor $\times$ Quotient $+$ Remainder
Here, Dividend $= 188$, Divisor $= 7$,
Quotient $= 26$ and Remainder $= 6$
In option (a), $(6 \times 26) + 7 = 163$
In option (b), $(26 \times 7) + 7 = 189$
In option (c), $(7 + 26) \times 6 = 198$
In option (d), $(7 \times 26) + 6 = 188$
So, option (d) is the correct answer.

8. According to the question,
(a)

Total ♟ in the city $= 6 \times 5 = 30$ men

Total ♀ in the city $= 5 \times 7 = 35$ women

So, total 5 women are more than men in the city.
$$[\because \text{required difference} = 35 - 30 = 5]$$

9. Louisa has 30 stickers, first we will find the
(b) stickers for each day.

Days	Martin	Louisa
1	4	6
2	$4 \times 2 = 8$	$6 \times 2 = 12$
3	$4 \times 3 = 12$	$6 \times 3 = 18$
4	$4 \times 4 = 16$	$6 \times 4 = 24$
5	$4 \times 5 = 20$	$6 \times 5 = 30$

From the given table, it is clear that Martin had 20 stickers when Louisa had 30 stickers.

10. 1-digit numbers $= 1 - 9 = 9$
(d) 2-digit numbers $= 11 - 99 = 90$

3-digit numbers $= 100 - 350 = 251$

So, number of digits used in numbering 350 pages of a book

$$= 1 \times \text{Number of 1-digit numbers}$$
$$+ 2 \times \text{Number of 2-digit numbers}$$
$$+ 3 \times \text{Number of 3-digit numbers}$$
$$= 1 \times 9 + 2 \times 90 + 3 \times 251$$
$$= 9 + 180 + 753 = 942$$

11. I. The number from which other number is
(d) subtracted is called <u>minuend</u>.

II. No number can be divided by <u>zero</u>.

III. When zero is subtracted from a number, the difference is the <u>number itself</u>.

IV. A <u>product</u> is the result of multiplication of two numbers.

12. Total marks in all the five subjects
(b) $$= 48 + 36 + 47 + 22 + 37 = 190$$

So, 190 is closest to 200.

13. Number of tickets Aryan had $= 132$
(b)
Number of people that can use 1 ticket $= 6$

$\therefore$ Total number of people that can use 132 tickets $= 132 \times 6 = 792$

14. I. $94 \times 6 = 564$ and $6 \times 94 = 564$
(c)
$\therefore 94 \times 6 = 6 \times 94$

II. $13 \times 9 + 6 = 123$

and $6 \times 9 + 13 = 67 \Rightarrow > 67$

$\therefore \qquad 13 \times 9 + 6 > 6 \times 9 + 13$

III. $0 \div 83 = 0$ and $83 \div 1 = 83$

$\Rightarrow \qquad 0 < 83$

$\therefore \qquad 0 \div 83 < 83 \div 1$

Hence, option (c) is correct.

15. I. True, any number multiplied by 1 is the
(d) number itself.

II. True, $165 + 332 = 497$

and $332 + 165 = 497$

III. False, subtraction is the inverse of addition.

IV. False, the number which is subtracted from the other number is called subtrahend.

Hence, option (d) is correct.

16. As per the question,
(d)
$$x - 2 + 6 + 3 = 12$$
$$\Rightarrow \qquad x - 2 + 9 = 12$$
$$\Rightarrow \qquad x + 7 = 12$$
$$\Rightarrow \qquad x = 12 - 7$$
$$\therefore \qquad x = 5$$

17. Total number of burgers $= 534$
(a)
Burger in each packet $= 6$

$\therefore$ Total number of packets required
$$= 534 \div 6 = 89$$

18. Flesh that tiger eat per day $= 9$ pounds
(a)
Weight of prey $= 315$ pounds

$\therefore$ Number of days food lasts $= 315 \div 9$
$$= 35$$

19. Number of goats in grazing field $= 60$
(c)
Total number of legs $= 60 \times 4 = 240$

$$[\because \text{goat has 4 legs}]$$

Number of deers in grazing field $= 30$

Total number of legs $= 30 \times 4 = 120$

$$[\because \text{deer has 4 legs}]$$

Number of children in grazing field $= 10$

Total number of legs $= 10 \times 2 = 20$

$$[\because \text{child has 2 legs}]$$

$\therefore$ Total number of legs $= 240 + 120 + 20$
$$= 380$$

20.
(a) Since,
$$72 \div h = 6 \qquad \Rightarrow \quad \frac{72}{h} = 6$$
$$\Rightarrow \quad h = \frac{72}{6} \qquad \Rightarrow \quad h = 72 \div 6 = 12$$
$\therefore$ Gary has 12 horses.

21.
(a) We have, LIV $\times$ XXV
where, L represents 50, IV represents 4, XX represents 20 and V represents 5)
So, we have
$$54 \times 25 = 1350 = \text{MCCCL}$$

22.
(a) Let the number be x.
As per the question,
$$x \times 85 + 187 - 22 = 3735$$
$$\Rightarrow \qquad 85x + 165 = 3735$$
$$\Rightarrow \qquad 85x = 3735 - 165$$
$$\Rightarrow \qquad 85x = 3570$$
$$\Rightarrow \qquad x = 3570 \div 85$$
$$\therefore \qquad x = 42$$

23.
(c) I. Greatest 3-digit number $+ 1 = 999 + 1$
$$\Rightarrow \qquad 1000 = \text{M}$$
II. 12 crore $-$ 15 lakh
$$= 120000000 - 1500000$$
$$= 118500000 = 1185 \text{ lakh}$$
III. 135 hundred $\times$ 5 hundred
$$= 13500 \times 500 = 6750000$$
$$= 675 \text{ ten thousand}$$
IV. CXXXV $+$ CXLII $= 135 + 142 = 277$
$$= \text{CCLXXVII}$$

24.
(c) According to the question,
Sum of numbers in both the diagonals is equal.
Diagonals numbers have been connected by arrows.

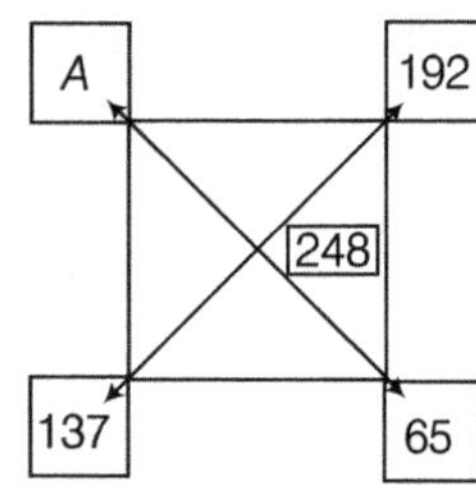

$\therefore \ 192 + 248 + 137 = A + 248 + 65$
$$\Rightarrow \qquad 577 = A + 313$$
$$\Rightarrow \qquad A = 577 - 313 = 264$$

25.
(c) Given,
Value of old fridge $= ₹\, 3250$
and money paid by Tanvi $= ₹\, 6329$
$\therefore$ Cost of TV that Tanvi bought
$$= ₹\, 6329 + ₹\, 3250 = ₹\, 9579$$

26.
(d) We have,
$$3 \otimes = 6$$
$$\Rightarrow \qquad 1 \otimes = 6 \div 3 = 2$$
$$2 \triangle + 1 \otimes = 8$$
$$\Rightarrow \qquad 2 \triangle = 8 - 2 = 6$$
$$\Rightarrow \qquad 1 \triangle = 6 \div 2 = 3$$
$$2 \square = 28$$
$$\Rightarrow \qquad 1 \square = 28 \div 2 = 14$$
$$4 \bigcirc = 64$$
$$\Rightarrow \qquad 1 \bigcirc = 64 \div 4 = 16$$
$\therefore \ 2 \otimes + 3 \triangle + 1 \bigcirc + 1 \square$
$$= 2 \times 2 + 3 \times 3 + 1 \times 16 + 1 \times 14$$
$$= 4 + 9 + 16 + 14 = 43$$

27.
(a) Given,
Cost of 2 teddy bears $= ₹\, 684$
$\Rightarrow$ Cost of 1 teddy bear $= ₹\, 684 \div 2 = ₹\, 342$
Cost of 2 scooters and 1 teddy bear $= ₹\, 1986$
$\Rightarrow$ Cost of 2 scooters
$$= ₹\, 1986 - \text{Cost of 1 teddy bear}$$
$$= ₹\, 1986 - ₹\, 342$$
$$= ₹\, 1644$$
$\therefore$ Cost of 1 scooter $= ₹\, 1644 \div 2 = ₹\, 822$
Cost of 1 car and 1 scooter $= ₹\, 2385$
$\Rightarrow$ Cost of 1 car $= ₹\, 2385 - \text{Cost of 1 scooter}$
$$= ₹\, 2385 - ₹\, 822$$
$$= ₹\, 1563$$
$\therefore$ Cost of 3 scooters $+$ Cost of 3 teddy bears
$$+ \text{ Cost of 2 cars}$$
$$= 3 \times ₹\, 822 + 3 \times ₹\, 342 + 2 \times ₹\, 1563$$
$$= ₹\, 2466 + ₹\, 1026 + ₹\, 3126$$
$$= ₹\, 6618$$

28.
(a) We have,
$$\begin{array}{r} 42859 \\ - 14X26 \\ \hline 27933 \\ \hline \end{array}$$
$$\Rightarrow \qquad 42859 - 27933 = 14X26$$
$$\Rightarrow \qquad 14926 = 14X26$$
On comparing both sides, we get $X = 9$

Mathematics Olympiad Class IV

29. Given,
$$27933$$
$$-11Y9$$
$$\overline{26774}$$

$\Rightarrow \qquad 27933 - 26774 = 11Y9$

$\Rightarrow \qquad\qquad\quad 1159 = 11Y9$

On comparing both sides, we get
$$Y = 5$$

30. If Cody throws, all the dart on circle with score 5, then score of Cody $= 5 \times 3 = 15$

If Cody throws all the dart on circle with score 6, then score of Cody $= 6 \times 3 = 18$

If Cody throws all the dart on circle with score 7, then score of Cody $= 7 \times 3 = 21$

$\Rightarrow$ Maximum score of Cody is 21.

So, 23 cannot be the score of Cody.

3 Factors and Multiples

1. 1 is the factor of every number.
(a)

2. Number of water bottles collected by Anna $= 8$
(b) Number of water bottles Raj collected
$$= \text{Twice as collected by Anna} = 2 \times 8 = 16$$
So, Raj had collected total 16 bottles.

3. To find the multiples of 9, first we recall the
(d) table of 9.

$9 \times 1 = 9 \qquad 9 \times 2 = 18$

$9 \times 3 = 27 \qquad 9 \times 4 = 36$

$9 \times 5 = 45 \qquad 9 \times 6 = 54$

$9 \times 7 = 63 \qquad 9 \times 8 = 72$

$9 \times 9 = 81$

So, it is clear that the numbers shown in option (d), i.e. 9, 18 and 45 are the multiples of 9.

4. In order to share pencils equally among three
(c) students, the number should be a multiple of 3.

Prashant has 13 pencils ; 13 is not a multiple of 3.

Radhika has 12 pencils ;
$$3 \times 4 = 12 \ (12 \text{ is a multiple of } 3)$$
Sonal has 19 pencils ; 19 is not a multiple of 3.

Neha has 15 pencils ;
$$3 \times 5 = 15 \ (15 \text{ is a multiple of } 3)$$
Hence, Radhika and Neha can share pencils equally among three students.

5. 6th multiple of $7 = 6 \times 7 = 42$
(c) 3rd multiple of $9 = 3 \times 9 = 27$

11th multiple of $12 = 11 \times 12 = 132$

$\therefore$ Required number $= 132 - (42 + 27)$
$$= 132 - 69 = 63$$

6. From the given expression, it is clear that 42 is
(d) 3 times as many as 14.

7. $\because 56 = 7 \times 8$ and $8 = 4 \times 2$
(a) $\therefore \qquad\qquad\qquad x = 8$

8. Every number is a factor and multiple of itself.
(d)

9. I. $\underline{3}$ is the smallest odd prime number.
(a) II. A number having more than $\underline{2}$ factors is called a composite number.

III. $\underline{1}$ is neither a prime number nor a composite number.

IV. The numbers having factor 2 and 3 also have factor $\underline{6}$.

Hence, option (a) is correct.

10. Multiples of 7 are 7, 14, 21 and 28.
(b) $\qquad\quad 7 = 1 \times 7; 24 = 2 \times 2 \times 2 \times 3$

$\therefore \quad \text{HCF} (7, 24) = 1$

$\qquad\quad 14 = 2 \times 7; \ 24 = 2 \times 2 \times 2 \times 3$

$\therefore \quad \text{HCF} (14, 24) = 2$

$\qquad\quad 21 = 3 \times 7; \ 24 = 2 \times 2 \times 2 \times 3$

$\therefore \quad \text{HCF} (21, 24) = 3$

and $\qquad\quad 28 = 2 \times 2 \times 7$

$\qquad\qquad\quad 24 = 2 \times 2 \times 2 \times 3$

$\therefore \qquad\quad \text{HCF} = (28, 24) = 4$

So, date chosen by Raghav $= 14$

[$\because$ 14 is multiples of 7 and the HCF of (14, 24) = 2]

11. Number shown in abacus is 343, which is a
(c) multiple of 7.

So, 7 is a factor of 343.

12. I. True, coprimes numbers have only one
(d) common factor, i.e. 1.

II. False, least prime number is 2.

III. True

IV. True

13. Only 432, i.e. the price of Computer Olympiad
(c) book is a multiple of 3 among all the four
prices of books, since $432 = 3 \times 144$

14. We have, factors of 10 are 1, 2, 5 and 10.
(a) Factors of 12 are 1, 2, 3, 4, 6 and 12.

Factors of $10 = 1, 2, 5$

Factors of $8 = 1, 2, 4, 8$

Factors of $15 = 1, 3, 5, 15$

From above factors, it is clear that 12 has 2 more factors than 10.

12 and 10 have 2 common factors, i.e. 1 and 2. The smallest possible value of X is 12.

15. The section B having any number which is a
(d) multiple of 20 but not a multiple of 10.

Here, 10 is a multiple of 10, 20 is a multiple of 10 and 20 both, 40 is also a multiple of 10 and 20 both.

Hence, option (d) is the correct answer.

16. $\because$ Dividend $=$ Divisor $\times$ Quotient $+$ Remainder
(c) $\therefore$ Required number $= 5 \times 8 + 3 = 40 + 3 = 43$
Hence, 43 is a prime number.

17. Here, the first lamppost below which a
(d) marking is made $=$ LCM (8, 12)

i.e. $\qquad 8 = 2 \times 2 \times 2, 12 = 2 \times 2 \times 3$

$\Rightarrow \qquad 2 \times 2 \times 2 \times 3 = 24$

Number of 24 m interval within 240 m long road $= 240 \div 24 = 10$

Number of markings $= 10 + 1 = 11$

Hence, there are 11 markings that are beside lampposts.

18. The number which is divisible by 2 and 5 and
(b) also closest to the 21st century.

1999 is not divisible by 2 and 5. 1990 is divisible by 2 and 5 both and also closest to the 21st century.

1995 is not divisible by 2 and 1998 is not divisible by 5.

Hence, option (b) is correct.

19. From Statement I, among the given options,
(c) (a) and (b) are not even numbers.

From Statement II, options (c) and (d) both are multiples of 6 and 7.

From Statement III, only 42 has total of 8 factors, i.e. 1, 2, 3, 6, 7, 14, 21, 42.

Hence, option (c) is correct.

20. Numbers between 20 and 30 are 21, 22, 23, 24,
(b) 25, 26, 27, 28, 29 and multiple of 4 are 24 and 28. When 24 is divided by 8, it leaves no remainder.

Hence, the required number is 24.

21. The smallest number which is a common
(c) multiple of 6 and 8 but not of 9 is 24.

$\therefore$ Required result $= 7 \times 5 + 24 = 35 + 24 = 59$

22. Statement I Predecessor of even numbers
(d) which are more than 80 but less than 100 are 81, 83, 85, 87, 89, 91, 93, 95, 97 and 99.

Statement II Numbers which are multiples of $3 = 81, 87, 93, 99$.

Statement III Numbers which are not a multiple of $11 = 81, 87, 93$.

Statement IV Number whose sum of digits is even $= 93$.

Hence, the number is 93.

23. Steps are as follow:
(b)
II. Greatest 4-digit number is 9999.

III. LCM of 15, 25, 40 and 75 is 600.

I. On dividing 9999 by 600, the remainder is 399.

IV. Number is $(9999 - 399) = 9600$.

So, the correct order is II, III, I, IV.

24. (a) Max is correct, as there are only 4 multiples
(b) of 8, i.e. 80, 40, 48, 24.

$\because 80 = 8 \times 10, 40 = 8 \times 5; 48 = 8 \times 6; 24 = 8 \times 3$

(b) Jeniffer is not correct, since 17, 11 and 2 are prime numbers.

(c) Rocky is correct, since (40, 11) are coprime numbers.

(d) Anjie is correct, since 11 is not even.

25. I. LCM (15, 30)
(b)
$\qquad 15 = 3 \times 5$ and $30 = 2 \times 3 \times 5$

i.e. $2 \times 3 \times 5 = 30$

II. LCM (8, 16)

$8 = 2 \times 2 \times 2$ and $16 = 2 \times 2 \times 2 \times 2$

i.e. $2 \times 2 \times 2 \times 2 = 16$, which is a factor of 64.

III. Factors of $2 = 1, 2$

Factors of $15 = 1, 3, 5, 15$

$\therefore$ Required sum $= 27$

IV. HCF (24, 6)

$\qquad 24 = 2 \times 2 \times 2 \times 3$ and $6 = 2 \times 3$

i.e. $2 \times 3 = 6$

26. Smallest three-digit number $= 100$
(c) $\therefore$ Divisor $= 100$

Quotient $=$ Successor of $100 = 101$

Remainder $=$ Predecessor of divisor $= 100 - 1 = 99$

$\therefore$ Dividend $=$ Divisor $\times$ Quotient $+$ Remainder

$\qquad = 100 \times 101 + 99 = 10100 + 99 = 10199$

Since, $10199 \div 7 = 1457$

Hence, 10199 is a multiple of 7.

27. Since, the day after which both the trucks will
(a) visit together $=$ LCM $(4, 5) = 4 \times 5 = 20$.

$\therefore$ Both the trucks will visit in 20 days.

28. The minimum amount of money Mr. Benrick
(c) must have spent on buying the children's and
adults' tickets $=$ LCM $(40, 70)$

As, $\qquad 40 = 2 \times 2 \times 2 \times 5$

and $\qquad 70 = 2 \times 5 \times 7$

$\therefore$ LCM $(40, 70) = 2 \times 2 \times 2 \times 5 \times 7 = ₹\,280$

29. Since, Jack has to cut the square shape with
(c) largest length.

$\therefore$ Jack will have to take HCF of length and
breadth to find the largest length.

$\qquad 42 = 2 \times 3 \times 7$

and $\qquad 27 = 3 \times 3 \times 3$

$\therefore$ HCF $(42, 27) = 3$

Hence, length of each square is 3 cm.

30. Since, $42 = 3 \times 14$ and $24 = 3 \times 9$
(b)

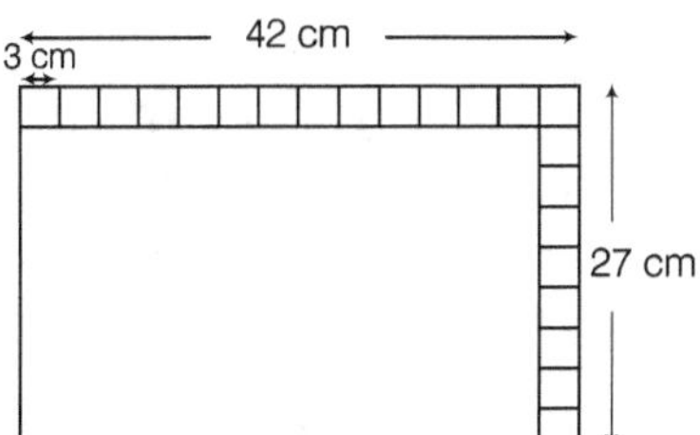

$\therefore$ Number of square shape papers $= 14 \times 9 = 126$

④ Fractions and Decimals

1. Total number of frogs $= 15$
(c)
Number of frogs hopped away $= 11$

Number of frogs left behind $= 15 - 11 = 4$

$\therefore$ Required fraction $= \dfrac{4}{15}$

2. In the given figure 6 parts are shaded out of
(b) 12 parts.

$\therefore$ Fraction of shaded part

$\qquad = \dfrac{\text{Number of shaded parts}}{\text{Total number of parts}} = \dfrac{6}{12}$

3. Given figure has 5 shaded parts out of 10.
(d) $\therefore$ Decimal fraction $= \dfrac{5}{10} = 0.5$

4. Number of matches played by $A = 10$
(b) Number of matches won by $A = 4$

Since, matches won by A are not exactly half
the matches he played.

Number of matches played by $B = 6$

Number of matches won by $B = 3$

Hence, it is clear that number of matches won
by B are exactly half the matches he played.

5. According to Rama, $\dfrac{2}{9}$ and $\dfrac{4}{18}$ are equivalent as
(c)
when $\dfrac{4}{18}$ is reduced to lowest fraction, its value
is $\dfrac{2}{9}$. So, Rama is correct.

Two fractions are equivalent when they have
same denominators, said by Asha is not correct.

According to Arjun, two fractions are equivalent
when they have the same value.

Thus, Arjun is also correct.

So, option (c) is correct answer.

6. In option (a), fraction $= \left(\dfrac{1}{2} + \dfrac{3}{2}\right) = \dfrac{4}{2}$
(a)
In option (b), fraction $= \left(\dfrac{2}{5} + \dfrac{2}{5}\right) = \dfrac{4}{5}$

In option (c), fraction $= \left(\dfrac{7}{9} + \dfrac{1}{9}\right) = \dfrac{8}{9}$

In option (d), fraction $= \left(\dfrac{12}{19} + \dfrac{6}{19}\right) = \dfrac{18}{19}$

Hence, all except option (a) has numerator 1 less
than denominator.

7. The given abacus represents

4 tens + 5 ones + 4 tenths + 5 hundredths

$$= 4 \times 10 + 5 \times 1 + 4 \times \frac{1}{10} + \frac{5}{100} = 45 + 0.45 = 45.45$$

8.
(a) The diagram represents 1 and $\frac{2}{20}$ part.

$$\therefore \text{ Required decimal} = 1 + \frac{2}{20} = 1 + \frac{1}{10} = 1.1$$

9.
(c) Arrange the given length of roads in ascending order

$$293.50 < 293.75 < 293.95 < 298.25.$$

[first compare whole parts. If they are same, then compare decimal parts]

So, the second largest road is built by 'Constructure Management'.

10.
(a) Alphabets made up of straight lines = 15

[first write all the alphabets on rough paper, then select the alphabets having only straight lines]

A, E, F, H, I, K, L, M, N, T, V, W, X, Y, Z.

Total number of alphabets = 26

$$\therefore \quad \text{Required fraction} = \frac{15}{26}$$

11.
(c) Given that sum of diagonals are equal.

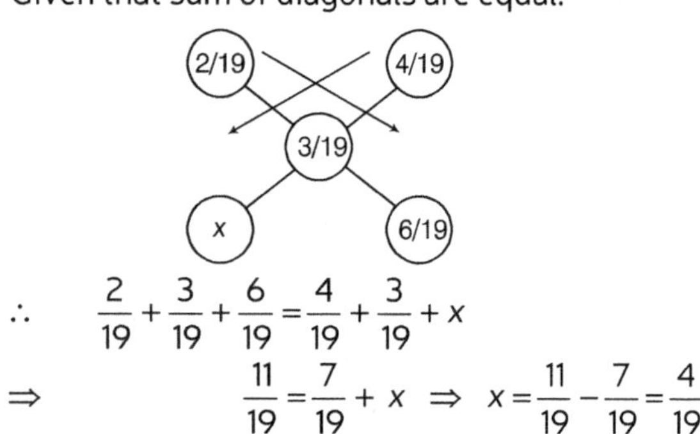

$$\therefore \quad \frac{2}{19} + \frac{3}{19} + \frac{6}{19} = \frac{4}{19} + \frac{3}{19} + x$$

$$\Rightarrow \quad \frac{11}{19} = \frac{7}{19} + x \Rightarrow x = \frac{11}{19} - \frac{7}{19} = \frac{4}{19}$$

12.
(d) In option (a), one-quarter $= \frac{1}{4}$ part is shaded.

In option (b), $2/8 = \frac{1}{4}$ part is shaded.

In option (c), $2/8 = \frac{1}{4}$ part is shaded.

In option (d), $\frac{4}{12} = \frac{1}{3}$ part is shaded.

13.
(c) Total number of cups of ingredients Jack used in making chocolate cake

$$= \frac{3}{4} + \frac{1}{2} + 2 + \frac{1}{8} + \frac{1}{10} + \frac{3}{4}$$

$$= \frac{30 + 20 + 80 + 5 + 4 + 30}{40}$$

$$= \frac{169}{40} = 4\frac{9}{40}$$

14.
(c) If we divide numerator and denominator both by 13, then $\frac{26}{65} \times \frac{13}{13} = \frac{2}{5}$.

If we divide both $\frac{104}{117}$ by 13, then it will become $\frac{8}{9}$.

Similarly, if we divide $\frac{91}{143} \times \frac{13}{13} = \frac{1183}{1859} = \frac{7}{11}$

Hence, option (c) is the correct answer.

15.
(d)
I. True

II. True

III. False, since we have travelled 15 miles which is half way. So, we have 15 miles to go.

IV. False, after eating three-fourth of pizza, only 1 part is left.

16.
(c)
I. $3.67 < 36.7$

II. $0.25 < 25.0$

III. $3.43 = 3.430$

17.
(b) P represents $= 2\frac{6}{10} = \frac{26}{10}$

Q represents $= 4\frac{3}{10} = \frac{43}{10}$

$$\therefore \quad Q - P = \frac{43}{10} - \frac{26}{10} = \frac{17}{10}$$

18.
(b) We have,

I. $\frac{56}{9} = 6\frac{2}{9}$ \qquad II. $\frac{37}{9} = 4\frac{1}{9}$

III. $\frac{23}{9} = 2\frac{5}{9}$ \qquad IV. $\frac{43}{9} = 4\frac{7}{9}$

19.
(a) According to the question,

$$\frac{5}{13} + x = 2$$

$$\Rightarrow \quad x = 2 - \frac{5}{13} = \frac{26 - 5}{13} = \frac{21}{13}$$

$$\text{and} \quad x + \frac{2}{13} = \frac{21}{13} + \frac{2}{13} = \frac{23}{13}$$

[∵ adding 2/13 on both sides]

$$\therefore \quad x = \frac{21}{13}$$

20.
(d) Given, score of Kelly = 58.93

and score of Karen = 74.92

∴ Required difference = 74.92 − 58.93

$$= 15.99$$

21. Length of one piece $= 1\dfrac{1}{5}$ metre $= \dfrac{6}{5}$ metre
(b)

Length of another piece $= 2\dfrac{2}{3} = \dfrac{8}{3}$ metre

$\therefore$ Total length of the bamboo rod $= \dfrac{6}{5} + \dfrac{8}{3}$

$$= \dfrac{18 + 40}{15} = \dfrac{58}{15} \text{ metre}$$

22. Car A will finish the race in $= \dfrac{3}{4} = 0.75$ minute
(c)

Car B will finish the race in $= \dfrac{7}{11} = 0.64$ minute

Car C will finish the race in $= \dfrac{7}{9} = 0.78$ minute

Car D will finish the race in $= \dfrac{5}{7} = 0.72$ minute

$\because \quad 0.64 < 0.72 < 0.75 < 0.78$

$\therefore \qquad B < D < A < C$

So, option (c) is the correct answer.

23. Fraction of the shaded portion of given
(a) image $= \dfrac{5}{8}$

In option (a), Fraction of unshaded portion $= \dfrac{5}{8}$

In option (b), fraction of unshaded portion $= \dfrac{6}{8}$

In option (c), fraction of unshaded portion $= \dfrac{7}{8}$

In option (d), fraction of unshaded portion $= \dfrac{4}{8}$

So, option (a) is the correct answer.

24. Price of meal $= ₹\,84$
(a)

Discount coupon $= \dfrac{3}{4}$

Discount available $= \dfrac{3}{4}$ of $84 = \dfrac{3}{4} \times 84$

$$= ₹\,63$$

$\therefore$ Price of meal $= 84 - 63 = ₹\,21$

25. Apples eaten by Shalini on Tuesday $= \dfrac{1}{9}$
(a)

Apples eaten by Shalini on Wednesday $= \dfrac{2}{9}$

Apples eaten by Shalini on Thursday $= \dfrac{2}{9}$

Remaining fraction of apples $= 1 - \left(\dfrac{1}{9} + \dfrac{2}{9} + \dfrac{2}{9} \right)$

$$= 1 - \dfrac{5}{9} = \dfrac{9 - 5}{9} = \dfrac{4}{9}$$

26. Value of one shaded area $= \dfrac{1}{4}$
(d)

The total similar equal part available in the given figure is 13.

So, $13 \times \dfrac{1}{4} = \dfrac{13}{4}$

5 Time and Calendar

1. Since, the hour hand is between 6 and 7 and
(c) minute hand is on 10. So, the clock shows $6:50$, which is same as $18:50$.

2. Time when rain started $= 10:07$ am
(c)

Time when rain stopped $= 3:15$ pm

$\therefore$ Elapsed time/Period of rainfall

$$= 3:15 \text{ pm} - 10:07 \text{ am}$$

$$= 5 \text{ hours } 8 \text{ minutes}$$

3. According to the given information,
(d)
(i) Kate and Suzanne have their birthdays in the same month, i.e. Kate and Suzanne have birthdays on June 15th and June 21st.

(ii) Julia and Suzanne have their birthdays on the same day of a month, i.e. on February 21st and June 21st.
Hence, Kate, Julia and Suzanne are not born on August 3rd.

So, Helena was born on August 3rd.

4. Expiry date of the given product
(b)
$$= 7/15$$
$$= \text{July } 2015$$

Manufacturing date of given product
$$= 5/14$$
$$= \text{May } 2014$$

$\therefore$ Elapsed time $= 1$ year and 2 months

5. Time in India $=12:53$ pm

(b) Time difference $=15$ hours

$\therefore$ Time in USA

$=$ Time in India $+$ Time difference

$=12:53$ pm $+15$ hours

$=12:53$ pm $+12$ hours $+3$ hours

$=12:53$ am $+3$ hours $=3:53$ am

6. Indian Standard Time $=2:55$ pm

(c) As per the given information,

Indian Standard Time $=$ Greenwich Mean Time
$$+5:30$$

$\Rightarrow$ Greenwich Mean Time

$=$ Indian Standard Time $-5:30$

$=2:55$ pm $-5:30=9:25$ am

7. Since, the year is 2012 and it is divisible by 4, so

(c) the year is a leap year.

$\therefore$ Number of days in February $=29$

and number of days in 2012 (leap year) $=366$

Hence, required fraction $=\dfrac{29}{366}$

8. Day on 1st July $=$ Monday

(a) Number of days in July $=31$

$\therefore$ Total number of days till 15th August
excluding 1st July $=30+15=45$

We know that, $45=7\times6+3$

Since, day repeats after 7 days, so it will be
Monday on 12th August,

Tuesday on 13th August,

Wednesday on 14th August

and Thursday on 15th August.

9. Given time $=3:50$ Quarter to $5=4:45$

(c) $\therefore$ Required time $=4:45-3:50=55$ minutes

After 55 more minutes, time will be $4:45$.

10. Time of sunrise $=5{:}52$ am

(c) Number of daylight hours $=13$ hours 32 minutes

$\therefore$ Time of sunset

$=5:52$ am $+13$ hours and 32 minutes

$=7:24$ pm

11. I. An year which is divisible by $\underline{4}$ is a leap year.

(a) II. 1 quarter hour $=15$ minutes

$\therefore$ 4 quarter hours $=4\times15$ minutes

$=60$ minutes $=\underline{1}$ hour

III. There are $\underline{7}$ months having 31 days, i.e. January, March, May, July, August, October, December.

IV. The time from 12 mid night to 12 noon is noted as $\underline{\text{am}}$.

12. Time at which Amelie completed baking the

(a) cake $=17:35$

Time used for baking $=2$ hours and 15 minutes

$\therefore$ Time at which she started baking

$=17:35-2$ hours 15 minutes $=15:20$

13. I. False, 3 hours $=3\times60\times60$ seconds

(d) $=10800$ seconds

and 14 minutes $=14\times60$ seconds

$=840$ seconds

$\therefore$ 3 hours 14 minutes

$=10800+840$ seconds $=11640$ seconds

II. False, $5:30$ pm is same as $17:30$.

III. False, 3 hours 49 minutes

-2 hours 58 minutes $=51$ minutes

IV. True

14. Given time $=6:20$ am

(d) Time taken in going from home to school
$=45$ minutes

Time taken in going from school to garden
$=18$ minutes

$\therefore$ Time taken in going from home to garden
$=(45+18)$ minutes $=63$ minutes

So, time at which Michael will reach garden
$=6:20$ am $+63$ minutes $=7:23$ am

15. $A=18:30$, $B=13:20$, $C=8:50$, $D=23:55$

(c)

16. As per the given information,

(a) Date on which Sally got new phone $=$ January 15

Number of days in 1 week and 5 days

$=(7+5)$ days $=12$ days

Today's date $=15$ January $+12$ days

$=27$th January

17. As given in the calendar, 17th May is Saturday

(d) and there are 31 days in the month of May.

Thus, next two Saturday will be on 24th and
31st May.

So, last Saturday will be on 31st May.

According to the given information, David went
to UK after six days from 31st May.

So, David went to UK on 6th June, 2008.

18. Birthday of Edda $= 12$th June
(c) Day on 28th March, 2015 $=$ Monday

Number of days from 28th March to 12th June
$[3 + 30 + 31 + 12] = 76$ days

So, $76 = 7 \times 11 - 1 =$ Monday $- 1$ day

$\therefore$ Day on Edda's birthday $=$ Sunday

19. Time at which Jessica arrived $= 8 : 12$ am
(d) Opening time of nursery on Tuesday $= 8 : 30$ am

Thus, Jessica will have to wait for
$8 : 30$ am $- 8 : 12$ am $= 18$ minutes.

20. Time taken by the wheel in going from one
(d) month to next month $= 2$ seconds

$\therefore$ Number of months covered in 30 seconds
$$= \frac{30}{2} = 15$$

So, starting from April and going
anti-clockwise, 15th month will be January.
Hence, wheel will stop on January.

21. Given time $= 5 : 20$ pm
(c) Colour of light $=$ red

Number of minutes traffic light stopped working
$$= 25 \text{ minutes}$$

Number of minutes traffic light takes to change
its colour $= 2$ minutes

$\therefore$ Light will become green after
$$= (25 + 2 + 2) \text{ minutes} = 29 \text{ minutes}$$

So, light will be green at
$5 : 20$ pm $+ 29$ minutes $= 5 : 49$ pm.

22. Time at which train reached Ajmer $= 6 : 00$ pm
(a) Travelling time $= 8$ hours

Waiting time at Shahdra station $= 10$ minutes

Arriving time at station after getting 1 hour

15 minutes late $= 6:00$ pm $-(8$ hours $+ 10$ minutes
$+ 1$ hour 15 minutes$) = 8 : 35$ am

23. First lesson of Sara $= 15$th March, Thursday
(a) Second lesson of Sara $= 18$th March, Sunday

Third lesson of Sara $= 21$st March, Wednesday

Fourth lesson of Sara $= 24$th March, Saturday

Fifth lesson of Sara $= 27$th March, Tuesday

Sixth lesson of Sara $= 30$th March, Friday

Hence, Sara will not have any class on Monday.

24. Time of leaving from London $= 2 : 20$ pm on
(b) Tuesday

Time of arriving in Sydney $= 6 : 40$ pm on
Wednesday

Time difference between London and Sydney
$$= 11 \text{ hours}$$

From the above information,

Time of arriving in Sydney as per the London
time $= 6 : 40$ pm Wednesday $- 11$ hours
$$= 7 : 40 \text{ am Wednesday}$$

$\therefore$ Duration of flight $= 2 : 20$ pm Tuesday
$$- 7 : 40 \text{ am Wednesday}$$
$$= 17 \text{ hours } 20 \text{ minutes}$$

25. Number of minutes Brenda's clock ahead
(c) $$= 20 \text{ minutes}$$

Alarm time $= 5 : 30$ am

Waiting time after snooze $= 7$ minutes

As per information, Brenda gets up when the
alarm rings for the third time.

So, the alarm snoozes for two time, i.e. for 14
minutes (7×2).

$\therefore$ Her alarm will ring third time at
$$(5 : 30 \text{ am} + 14 \text{ minutes}) = 5 : 44 \text{ am}$$

Since, her clock is 20 minutes ahead, then actual
time is $5 : 44$ am $- 20$ minutes $= 5 : 24$ am

So, Brenda will get up at $5 : 24$ am.

6 Money

1. Given, $\dfrac{1}{4}$ of $\rupee\, x = 25$ paise $\Rightarrow \dfrac{1}{4} \times \rupee\, x = \rupee\, \dfrac{25}{100}$
(a)
$$\therefore \qquad x = \rupee\, \frac{25 \times 4}{100} = \rupee\, 1$$

2. $7.00 = \underline{14} \times 50$ paise
(b)
Option (a), 10×50 paise $= \rupee\, 5$ $[\because 100$ paise $= \rupee\, 1]$

Option (b), 14×50 paise $= \rupee\, 7$

Option (c), 20×50 paise $= \rupee\, 10$

Option (d), 24×50 paise $= \rupee\, 12$

3. We have,
(c) Option (a), 280 paise $= \rupee\, 2.80$
$$[\because \rupee\, 1 = 100 \text{ paise}]$$

Option (b), $\rupee\, 4.85$

Option (c), 5×25 paise $= \rupee\, 1.25$

Option (d), Twenty 10 paise coins
$$20 \times 0.10 = \rupee\, 2$$

So, option (c) has least value.

4. Given, money received by Jack = £ 20
(d) and £ 1 = $ 1.74

$\therefore$ £ 20 = $ 20 × 1.74 = $34.80

5. Option (a), 4 × 2 + 1 × 1 + 1 × 0.25
(a)

$= ₹ 8 + ₹ 1 + ₹ 0.25 = ₹ 9.25$

Option (b), 4 × 2 + 1 × 0.50 + 1 × 0.25

$= ₹ 8 + ₹ 0.50 + ₹ 0.25 = ₹ 8.75$

Option (c), 1 × 5 + 12 × 0.50 = ₹ 5 + ₹ 6 = ₹ 11

Option (d), 1 × 5 + 2 × 1 + 6 × 0.25

$= ₹ 5 + ₹ 2 + ₹ 1.5 = ₹ 8.5$

Hence option (a) is the correct answer.

6. I. True
(c) II. False, ₹ 5.75 means five hundred seventy five paise.

III. False, there are 400 twenty five paise coins in ₹ 100.

IV. True, the given amount is equal to ₹ 14.85.

7. Cost of cricket bat = ₹ 180
(c) Money Bunny had = ₹ 500

$\therefore$ Money left with Bunny

= Total money − Money spent on cricket bat

= ₹ 500 − ₹ 180 = ₹ 320

8. Price of 1 bouquet = ₹ 50
(a) Number of flowers in 1 bouquet = 10

$\therefore$ Number of bouquet made out of 600 flowers

$$= \frac{600}{10} = 60$$

$\therefore$ Price of 60 bouquet = ₹ 50 × 60

$= ₹ 3000$

9. I. 500 paise makes <u>5</u> rupees.
(d) II. <u>250</u> paise makes two and a half rupee.

III. $\frac{3}{4}$ of 1 rupee = $\frac{3}{4}$ × 100 paise = <u>75</u> paise

IV. Cost of 1 cup of tea = ₹ 6.

$\therefore$ Cost of 5 cups of tea = ₹ 6 × 5 = ₹ <u>30</u>

10. Fine for 1st day = ₹ 1
(c) Fine for 2nd day = ₹ 1

Fine for 3rd day = ₹ 2

Fine for 4th day = ₹ 3

$\therefore$ Total fine for 4 days = 3 + 2 + 1 + 1 = ₹ 7

11. Given, cost of the book = ₹ 192.65
(a) $\therefore$ Fine that library charges = 2 × Cost of book

$= 2 × ₹ 192.65$

$= ₹ 385.30$

12. Number of hours Christina worked = 15 hours
(b) Money earned in 1 hour = ₹ 100

Money earned in 15 hours = ₹ 100 × 15 = ₹ 1500

Money spent = $\frac{1}{4}$ th of ₹ 1500

$$= \frac{1}{4} × 1500 = ₹ 375$$

$\therefore$ Money left with Christina = ₹ 1500 − ₹ 375

$= ₹ 1125$

13. **Option** (a), Cost of bow = ₹ 50
(c) Cost of winter cap = ₹ 75

$\therefore$ Cost of bow and winter cap = ₹ 50 + ₹ 75

$= ₹ 125$

Total money Anna had = ₹ 100

So, Statement (a) is incorrect.

Option (b), Cost of pair of gloves = ₹ 450

Money Anna had = ₹ 250

So, Statement (b) is incorrect.

Option (c), Cost of a bow = ₹ 50

Cost of two bows = ₹ 2 × 50 = ₹ 100

Cost of winter cap = ₹ 75

Cost of a purse = ₹ 200

$\therefore$ Total cost of two bows, a winter cap and a purse = ₹ 200 + ₹ 75 + ₹ 100 = ₹ 375

Total money Suzanne had = ₹ 500

She can buy two bows, a winter cap and a purse.

Hence , option (c) is the correct answer.

14. I. ₹ 48 ÷ ₹ 3 = ₹ 16
(d) II. 16 × 25 paise = 400 paise = ₹ 4

III. ₹ 23.25 − ₹ 6.95 = ₹ 16.30

IV. ₹ 19.65 − 25 paisa = ₹ 19.65 − ₹ 0.25

$= ₹ 19.40$

15. **Option** (a), Cost of 2 candy bars = ₹ 5.90
(c) $\therefore$ Cost of 1 candy bar = ₹ 5.90 ÷ 2 = ₹ 2.95

Option (b), Cost of 6 candy bars = ₹ 19.5

$\therefore$ Cost of 1 candy bar = ₹ 19.5 ÷ 6 = ₹ 3.25

Option (c), Cost of 4 candy bars $= ₹\,4.76$

$\therefore$ Cost of 1 candy bar $= ₹\,4.76 \div 4 = ₹\,1.19$

Option (d) is cannot be determined.

So, 4 candy bars for $₹\,4.76$ is a better buy.

Hence, option (c) is correct.

16. I. 560 paise $= ₹\,5.60$
(d)
$\qquad \therefore ₹\,5.60 < ₹\,7.80$

II. $\dfrac{2}{3}$ of $₹\,9 = \dfrac{2}{3} \times 9 = ₹\,6$ and 600 paise $= ₹\,6$

$\qquad \therefore \dfrac{2}{3}$ of $₹\,9 = 600$ paise

III. 7 one rupee note $= ₹\,7$

10 fifty paise coins $= ₹\,10 \times 0.50 = ₹\,5$

Thus, 7 one rupee note $>$ 10 fifty paise coins.

IV. 6 rupees and 25 paise $= ₹\,6.25$

5 rupee and 200 paise $= ₹\,5 + ₹\,2 = ₹\,7$

So, 6 rupees and 25 paise $<$ 5 rupee and 200 paise.

17. Money saved by Hannu in 1st week $= ₹20$
(d)
Money saved by Hannu in 2 weeks $= ₹60$

$\qquad (₹\,40 + ₹\,20)$

Money saved by Hannu in 3 week $= ₹120$

$\qquad (₹\,40 + ₹\,20 + ₹\,60)$

Money saved by Hannu in 4 weeks

$\qquad = ₹\,120 + ₹\,80 = ₹\,200$

Hence, after 4 weeks, Hannu will be able to buy the videogame.

18. Savings of Kia $= ₹\,415$
(a)
As per the given information,

Kia has four $₹\,10$ notes, twenty five $₹\,1$ note

$\qquad = 4 \times ₹\,10 + 25 \times ₹\,1 = ₹\,(40 + 25) = ₹\,65$

$\therefore$ Money left $= ₹\,415 - ₹\,65 = ₹\,350$

$\therefore$ Number of notes of $₹\,50 = ₹\,350 \div ₹\,50 = 7$

19. Cost of 1 pen $= ₹\,17.75$
(c)
$\therefore$ Cost of 5 pens $= 17.75 \times 5 = ₹\,88.75$

Money left with Stella $= ₹\,15.95$

$\therefore$ Money which Stella had

$\qquad = $ Money spent $+$ Money left

$\qquad = ₹\,88.75 + ₹\,15.95$

$\qquad = ₹\,104.70$

20. Tessie had $= 15$ kg newspaper
(d)
Amount Tessie received $= ₹\,6 \times 15 = ₹\,90$

Adira had $= 13$ kg plastic

Amount Adira received $= ₹\,12 \times 13 = ₹\,156$

Tulip had $= 2$ kg iron and 4 kg brass

$\qquad = 2 \times ₹\,14 + 4 \times ₹\,180$

$\qquad = ₹\,28 + ₹\,720 = ₹\,748$

$\therefore$ Total amount Ragman paid

$\qquad = ₹\,748 + ₹\,156 + ₹\,90 = ₹\,994$

So, Statement (d) is correct while other statements are incorrect.

21. Charge for first kilometre $= ₹\,8$
(d)
Charge for the successive kilometre $= ₹\,10$

Distance travelled by Rex $= 58$ km

$\therefore$ Total money Rex had to pay

$\qquad = ₹\,8 \times 1 + ₹\,10 \times 58$

$\qquad = ₹\,588$

22. Price of 1 shirt $= ₹\,125.75$
(d)
Money I had $= ₹\,754.50$

$\therefore$ Number of shirts bought $= \dfrac{754.50}{125.75} = 6$

Since, one shirt is free with two.

So, I will get 3 shirts more on purchase of 6 shirts.

$\therefore$ Total shirts bought $= 6 + 3 = 9$

23. Total cost of 4 toy cars and 6 cookies $= ₹\,572$
(a)
As per the given information,

Cost of 1 toy car $= ₹\,38 +$ Cost of 1 cookie

$\Rightarrow$ Cost of 4 toy cars

$\qquad = 4 \times (₹\,38 +$ Cost of 1 cookie$)$

$\qquad = ₹\,152 +$ Cost of 4 cookies

$\therefore$ Cost of 6 cookies $+$ Cost of 4 toy cars

$\qquad = ₹\,572$

$\Rightarrow$ Cost of 6 cookies $+ ₹\,152 +$ Cost of 4 cookies

$\qquad\qquad = ₹\,572$

$\Rightarrow$ Cost of 10 cookies $= ₹\,572 - ₹\,152$

$\qquad\qquad = ₹\,420$

$\Rightarrow$ Cost of 1 cookie $= ₹\,420 \div 10 = ₹\,42$

24. Cost of 1 ticket for boys $= ₹\,200$
(c)
Cost of 2 ticket for boys $= ₹\,2 \times 200 = ₹\,400$

As per question, $\dfrac{1}{4}$ th is off on girls entry.

Cost of 1 ticket for a girl $= 200 - \dfrac{1}{4}$ th $\times 200$

$\qquad = ₹\,200 - ₹\,50 = ₹\,150$

Cost of 2 tickets for girls $= 2 \times ₹\,150 = ₹\,300$

Money spent on food = ₹ 200

Money spent on travelling = ₹ 50

∴ Total money spent = Money spent on tickets
+ Money spent of food + Money spent on
travelling

= ₹ 400 + ₹ 300 + ₹ 200 + ₹ 50 = ₹ 950

∴ Share of each friend = ₹ 950 ÷ 4 = ₹ 237.50

25. ₹ 1 = € 0.014
(b) ⇒ ₹ 280000 = ₹ 280000 × € 0.014 = € 3920

So, Ann has € 3920 in Spain.

Money spent by Ann in Spain = € 450

Money left = € 3920 − € 450 = € 3470

Now, € 1 = $ 1.13

⇒ € 3470 = € 3470 × $ 1.13 = $ 3921.1

Thus, Ann has $ 3921.1 in france.

Money spent in france = $ 352

Money left = $3921.1 − $352 = $ 3569.1

Given, $ 1 = ₹ 62.5

⇒ $ 3569.1 = $ 3569.1 × ₹ 62.5

= ₹ 223068.75

⑦ Measurement

1. Correct order is II < IV < I < III.
(d) Since, spoon holds lesser quantity than all. A cup
will hold less quantity than kettle and bucket.
Kettle holds lesser quantity than bucket finally
bucket will hold highest quantity among all.

2. All except potatoes are measured in litre or
(c) millilitre.

3. The length of the given object is 3 cm and 3 mm
(c) which is equal to 3.3 cm or 3 cm 3 mm.

4. I. True
(b)
II. False, long distances are measured in
kilometre.

III. True

IV. True

5. I. Length of a football field is measured with the
(b) help of inch tape.

II. Weight of a kilogram of meat is measured with
the help of weighing machine.

III. Length of a paper clip is measured with the
help of ruler.

IV. Volume of milk is measured with the help of
measuring flask.

6. I. Correct
(d)
II. Correct

III. Correct

IV. Incorrect, hectogram is bigger unit than
decagram.

7. Here, $AD = 3$ cm, $EF = 1$ cm, $HJ = 2$ cm
(b)
∴ $AD + EF + HJ = 3$ cm + 1 cm + 2 cm = 6 cm

and $AF = 5$ cm, $DJ = 6$ cm, $CG = 4$ cm,
$EJ = 5$ cm

Hence, $AD + EF + HJ = DJ$

8. I. $8 × 1000$ g = 8000 g = 8 kg
(a)
II. 900 g + 100 g = 1000 g = 1 kg

III. 4000 g ÷ 4 = 1000 g = 1 kg

IV. 780 g − 280 g = 500 g = 0.5 kg

Hence, option (a) is the correct answer.

9. Volume of lemonade = 400 mL
(c) Volume of lemonade Moishe drank

$$= \frac{1}{4} \text{ of } 400 \text{ mL}$$

$$= 100 \text{ mL}$$

Volume of lemonade left

= Total volume − Volume drank

= 400 mL − 100 mL = 300 mL

10. I. The standard unit of volume or capacity
(b) is <u>litre</u>.

II. 1000 mg = <u>1g</u>

III. Very light weights are measured in
<u>milligram</u>.

IV. 1 km is <u>1000</u> times 100 cm.

11. Measure of 1 hand = 4 inch
(c)
Height of horse = 14 hands

Measure of 14 hands = 14 × 4 inch = 56 inch

∴ Height of a horse = 56 inch

12. Weight on 1st pan = 750 g
(a)
To balance both the pan, first convert the
kilogram (kg) into gram (g).

Mathematics Olympiad Class IV

Weight on 2nd pan $= 2\,kg = 2000\,g$

In order to balance the scales, weight on 1st pan must be equal to the weight on 2nd pan.

$\therefore$ Weight needed to add on 1st pan

$$= 2000\,g - 750\,g$$
$$= 1250\,g$$

13. The given distance between Aaron and his
(b) Grandma's house $= 5300\,m$

Length of long route $= 9.2\,km \qquad [\because 1\,km = 100\,m]$
$$= 9.2 \times 1000\,m = 9200\,m$$

Required difference $= 9200\,m - 5300\,m$
$$= 3900\,m = (3900 \div 1000)\,km = 3.9\,km$$

14. Number of patients $= 14$
(c) Volume of syrup $= 1190\,mL$

$\Rightarrow$ Volume of syrup given to each patient
$$= 1190\,mL \div 14 = 85\,mL$$

15. Volume of water in a tank $= 1.5\,kL$
(d)
$$= 1.5 \times 1000\,L = 1500\,L$$
Volume of bucket $= 125\,L$

$\therefore$ Number of buckets required to empty the tank
$$= 1500\,L \div 125\,L = 12$$

16. Since, in border X, 16 small rope piece of 1 cm
(c) needed to make the border. In same way, 10 small rope piece of 1 cm needed to make the border. Hence, length of the border
$$Y = 10 \times 1\,cm = 10\,cm$$

17. Length of Kelsey's pencil box $= 16\,cm$
(b) As per the question,

Length of Hanna's pencil box
$$= \text{Length of Kelsey's pencil box} - 4\,cm$$
$$= 16\,cm - 4\,cm = 12\,cm$$

and, length of Mark's pencil box
$$= \text{Length of Hanna's pencil box} + 2\,cm$$
$$= 12\,cm + 2\,cm = 14\,cm$$

18. Given,
(b) Total volume of petrol required by Danny excluding Thursday
$$= 240\,mL + 560\,mL + 385\,mL$$
$$+ 358\,mL + 237\,mL$$
$$= 1780\,mL = 1.78\,L \qquad [\because 1\,L = 100\,mL]$$
and volume of petrol required in entire week
$$= 2180\,mL = 2.18\,L$$
$\therefore$ Volume of petrol required on Thursday
$$= 2.18\,L - 1.78\,L = 0.40\,L = 400\,mL$$

19. Length of each step of Smith $= 75\,cm$
(c) Total number of steps taken by Smith $= 20000$

$\therefore$ Distance covered in 20000 steps
$$= 20000 \times 75\,cm$$
$$= 1500000 = 15\,km$$

Given, $1\,mile = 1.6\,km$
$$\Rightarrow \qquad 1\,km = \frac{1}{1.6}\,miles$$
$$\Rightarrow \qquad 15\,km = 15 \times \frac{1}{1.6}\,miles = 9.375\,miles$$

20. Given,
(b) Weight of 3 books + Weight of 1 puppy
$$= 12\,kg$$
As can be seen in the diagram given in question,

Weight of 3 books $=$ Weight of puppy

$\Rightarrow$ Weight of 3 books $= 12\,kg \div 2 = 6\,kg$

$[\because$ there are two elements, i.e. book and puppy$]$

$\therefore$ Weight of 1 book $= 6\,kg \div 3 = 2\,kg$

21. Given, volume of 10 cups of water
(a)
$$= \text{Volume of jug} \div 2$$
$\Rightarrow$ Volume of 10 cups of water $= 4\,L \div 2$

$\therefore$ Volume of 1 cup of water $= 2\,L \div 10$
$$= 2000\,mL \div 10 \qquad [\because 2\,L = 2000\,mL]$$
$$= 200\,mL$$

22. Weight of 2 apples $= 20\,g$
(b) $\therefore$ Weight of 1 apple $= 10\,g$

Weight of 2 mangoes and 1 apple $= 46\,g$

$\Rightarrow$ Weight of 2 mangoes $= 46\,g - 10\,g = 36\,g$

$\therefore$ Weight of 1 mango $= 36\,g \div 2 = 18\,g$

and weight of 1 mango and 1 pear $= 24\,g$

$\therefore$ Weight of 1 pear $= 24\,g - 18\,g = 6\,g$

23. Length of bridge $= 600\,m$
(c) Length of truck $= 5\,m$

Gap between trucks $= 1\,m$

$\therefore$ Total length required by 1 truck
$$= \text{Length of a truck} + \text{Gap between trucks}$$
$$= 5\,m + 1\,m = 6\,m$$

So, number of trucks that can stand on the bridge $= 600\,m \div 6\,m = 100\,trucks$

24. Length of gift $= 38\,cm$
(b) Length of wrapping paper $= 64\,cm$

Margin to be left on both sides
$$= 5\,cm + 5\,cm = 10\,cm$$

∴ Length of wrapping paper left

$$= 64 \text{ cm} - (38 \text{ cm} + 10 \text{ cm})$$
$$= 64 \text{ cm} - 48 \text{ cm} = 16 \text{ cm}$$

25. Volume of oil in bottles A and B
(c)
$$= 3 \text{ L } 400 \text{ mL} + 1 \text{ L } 650 \text{ mL}$$
$$= 3400 \text{ mL} + 1650 \text{ mL}$$
$$= 5050 \text{ mL} = 5 \text{ L } 50 \text{ mL}$$

Volume of oil in bottles B and C
$$= 1 \text{ L } 650 \text{ mL} + 3 \text{ L } 925 \text{ mL}$$
$$= 1650 \text{ mL} + 3925 \text{ mL}$$
$$= 5575 \text{ m}$$
$$= 5 \text{ L } 575 \text{ mL}$$

Volume of oil in bottles C and A
$$= 3 \text{ L } 925 \text{ mL} + 3 \text{ L } 400 \text{ mL}$$
$$= 3925 \text{ mL} + 3400 \text{ mL}$$
$$= 7325 \text{ mL}$$
$$= 7 \text{ L } 325 \text{ mL}$$

∴ Volume of oil in bottles B and D
$$= 1 \text{ L } 650 \text{ mL} + 2 \text{ L } 692 \text{ mL}$$
$$= 1650 \text{ mL} + 2692 \text{ mL}$$
$$= 4342 \text{ mL}$$
$$= 4 \text{ L } 342 \text{ mL}$$

Hence, option (c) is the correct answer.

26. Given,
(c)

$$10 \; \square + 10 \; \square + 10 \; \triangle = 3200 \text{ g}$$

$$\Rightarrow 1 \; \square + 1 \; \square + 1 \; \triangle = \frac{3200}{10} = 320 \text{ g} \quad \text{...(i)}$$

Now, $\triangle = \square - 20 \text{g} \qquad \text{...(ii)}$

and $\square = 70 \text{ g} + \square \qquad \text{...(iii)}$

Now, putting the values in Eq. (i), we get

$$\Rightarrow \square + 70 \text{ g} + \square + \square - 20 \text{ g} = 320 \text{ g}$$

$$\Rightarrow 3 \; \square = 270 \text{ g}$$

$$\Rightarrow \square = 90 \text{ g} \qquad \text{...(iv)}$$

Now, $\triangle = \square - 20 \text{ g} \qquad$ [from Eq. (ii)]

$$\Rightarrow \triangle = 90 \text{ g} - 20 \text{ g} = 70 \text{ g} \qquad \text{[from Eq. (iv)]}$$

(8) Geometry

1. Line segments in the given figure are
(c) $\overline{AB}, \overline{BC}, \overline{CD}, \overline{DE}, \overline{EF}, \overline{FG}, \overline{GH}, \overline{HI}, \overline{IJ}, \overline{JA}, \overline{OA}, \overline{OB},$
$\overline{OC}, \overline{OD}, \overline{OE}, \overline{OF}, \overline{OG}, \overline{OH}, \overline{OI}, \overline{OJ}.$

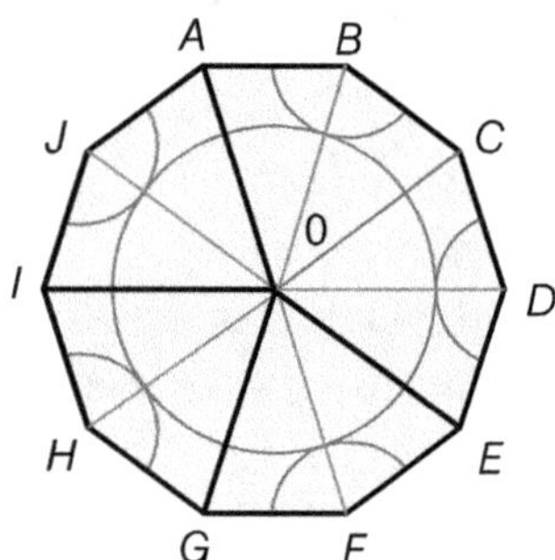

∴ There are 20 line segments.

2. (a) → Tip of a pencil is an example of a point.
(c)
(b) → Equator line is an example of a line because it is infinite.

(c) → Flashlight is an example of a ray, since it originates from torch/headlight and extends infinitely from the other side.

(d) → Edges of paper is an example of a line segment because its length is fixed.

Hence, option (c) is correct.

3. The angle between prime Meridian and axis of
(a) the Earth is less than 90° and hence it is an acute angle.

4. Given figure consists of 5 circles.
(d)

5. I. The hands of the first clock are inclined at
(c) an angle less than 90°. Hence, they form an acute angle.

II. The hands of the second clock are inclined at an angle greater than 90°.

Hence, they form an obtuse angle.

III. The hands of the third clock are inclined at 90°. Hence, they form a right angle.

So, option (c) is the correct answer.

6. (c) In a polygon, minimum number of sides can be three and a polygon with three sides is called a triangle.

7. (c) A polygon with five sides is called a pentagon. Hence, the given diagram of tile shows a pentagon inside a square.

8. (d) Number of triangles in figure (a) = 5

Number of triangles in figure (b) = 5

Number of triangles in figure (c) = 5

Hence, all the tangrams have equal number of triangles, i.e. 5.

9. (c) The given objects have the shape of a cylinder.

10. (b) There are 11 alphabets which are made up of curved lines, i.e. B, C, D, G, J, O, P, Q, R, S, U.

11. (d) The given figure consists of 8 edges, i.e. $\overline{AB}, \overline{BC}, \overline{CD}, \overline{DE}, \overline{EB}, \overline{AC}, \overline{AD}, \overline{AE}$.

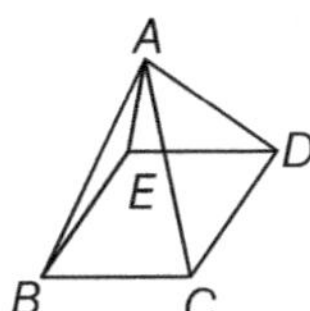

12. (a) If we joined all points, we will gets line segments AB, BC, CD, DA, AC, BD.

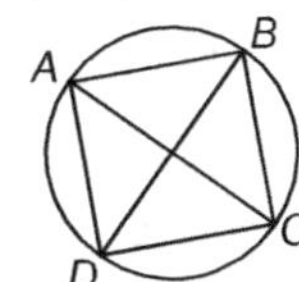

Hence, total number of line segments are 6.

13. (d) Any four sided figure with sides not necessarily of the same length is a quadrilateral.

e.g. 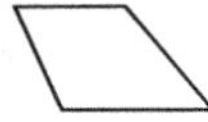

14. (b) The correct arrangement of steps are CADB.

15. (b) I. Only <u>one</u> line can pass through two distinct points.

II. <u>Diameter</u> is twice the radius of circle.

III. An angle less than 90° is an <u>acute</u> angle.

IV. A <u>chord</u> is a line segment that connects any two points on the circle.

16. (b) Since, PQ and PR are radii of the same circle. Thus, length of PQ and PR are equal.

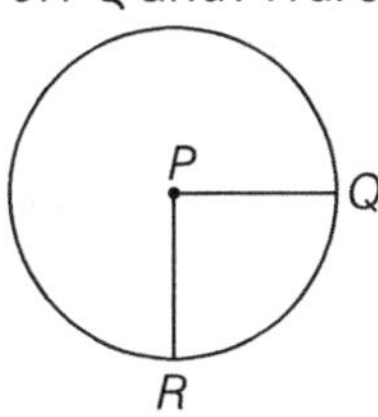

From the above diagram, it is clear that P is the centre of the circle and Q, R are points on the circle. But PQ is not a chord of the circle, because a chord joins two points on the circle.

17. (c) Pentagon consists of 5 angles.

18. (a) I. False, no two lines can intersect at more than one point.

II. True

III. True, a cuboid is made up of 6 rectangles.

IV. False, in a ΔPQR, vertices are P, Q and R.

19. (d) The given figure consists of two right angles, one acute angle and one obtuse angle.

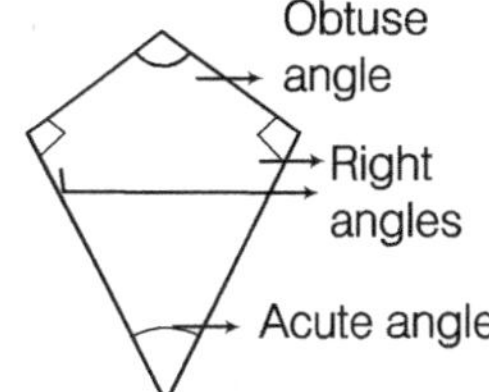

20. (b) The shapes with their nets are given below:

(i) 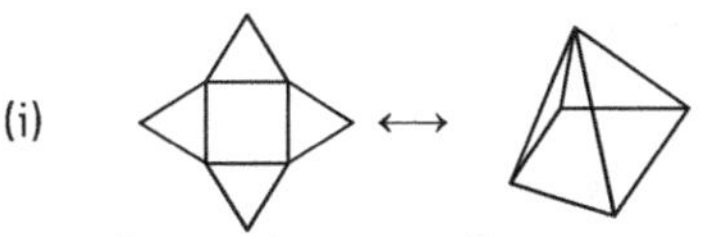

(ii) 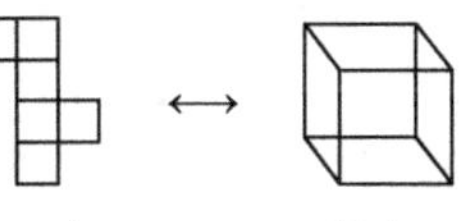

(iii) 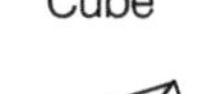

(iv) 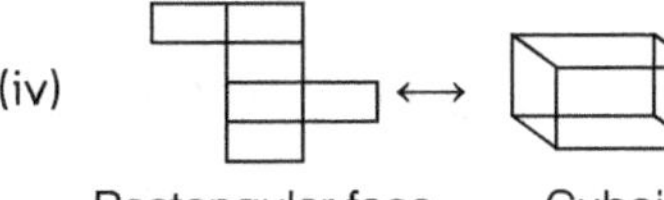

21. Figure (a) has 2 faces.
(b) Figure (b) has 6 faces.
Figure (c) has 1 face.
Figure (d) has 4 faces.
∴ Only figure (b) consists of exactly 6 faces.

22. The figures after joining are as shown below :
(c)

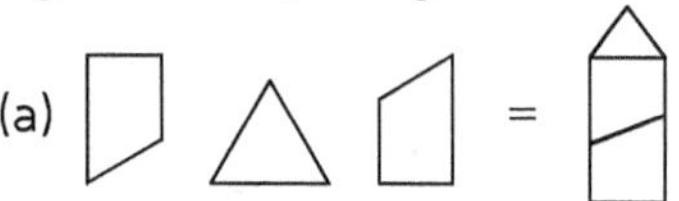

Hence, figures shown in option (c) make a rectangle when they all are joint together.

23. I. A four sided figure with straight edges can be
(d) square or rectangle. But as given in the statement, figure is not square.
Thus, it is a rectangle.

II. Only cone consists of one curved surface, one flat surface and one edge.
So, it is a cone.

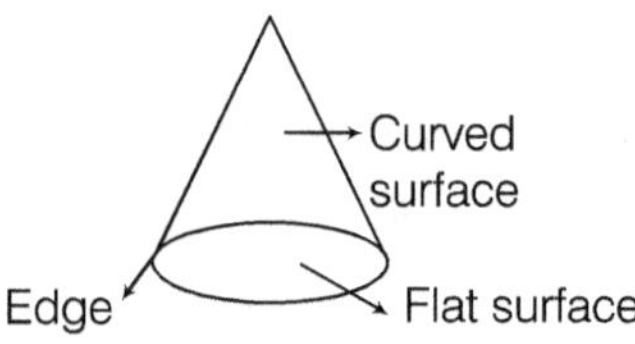

III. Sphere is a shape with no corners, no edges and only one curved surface.
Therefore, it is a sphere .

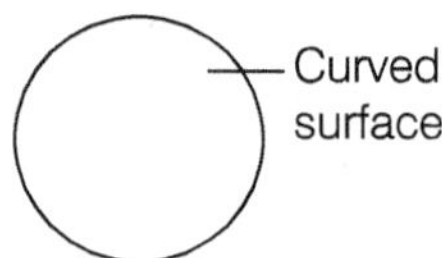

IV. A triangle consists of three corners with three angles, one out of which can be a right angle. So, it is a triangle.

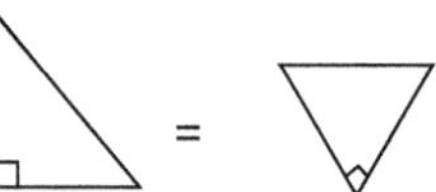

Hence, option (d) is correct.

⑨ Area and Perimeter

1. Perimeter of $\triangle PQR$
(c)
$$= PQ + QR + RP$$
$$[\because \text{perimeter of triangle = sum of all sides}]$$
$$= 5\,cm + 3\,cm + 7.8\,cm = 15.8\,cm$$

2. I. False, area is expressed in square units.
(b) II. False, area is measured in square units, while perimeter in measured in units only.
III. False, triangle is a three sided polygon, while quadrilateral is a four sided polygon.
IV. True

3. I. <u>Perimeter</u> is expressed in units of length.
(c) II. Perimeter of a triangle with sides a, b and c is <u>$a + b + c$</u>.
III. Perimeter of a regular hexagon is <u>$6 \times$ sides</u>.
IV. Area of 15 unit squares is <u>15</u> sq units.

4. Field is in the shape of a square whose side is
(a) 24 m.
∴ Area in which cow can graze = Side × Side
$$= (24 \times 24)\,m^2 = 576\,m^2$$

5.
(d)

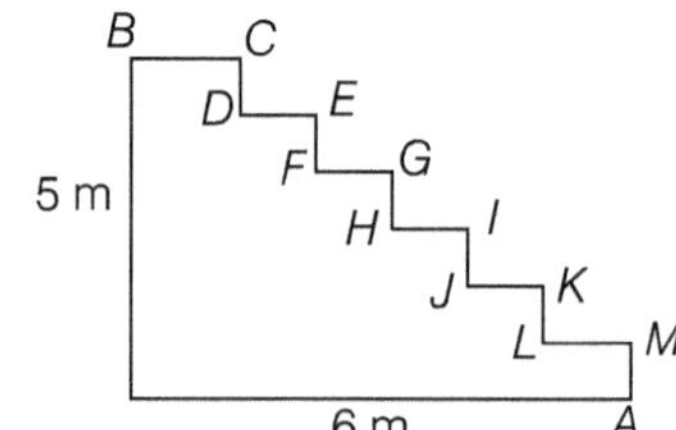

The distance covered by ant from A to B is as follows
$$AM + LK + JI + HG + FE + DC = 5\,m$$
and $\quad BC + DE + FG + HI + JK + LM = 6\,m$
∴ The ant crawls $= (5 + 6) = 11\,m$

6. Both Raven and Rosy have same starting and
(a) ending point and Raven runs faster than Rosy yet she loses the race, because perimeter of outer circle or track is more than the perimeter of inner circle or track.

7. Given, length $= 12$ cm and breadth $= 10$ cm
(c) $\therefore$ Area of rectangle $=$ Length $\times$ Breadth
$$= (12 \times 10)\,cm^2 = 120\,cm^2$$
So, area of each piece $= (120 \div 4)\,cm^2 = 30\,cm^2$

8. Perimeter $=$ Sum of all sides $= 28$ units,
(c) When the left out square is placed at C, the perimeter will get reduced by 4 units. Since, the position of C square bounded by all four sides.

9. Option (b) is correct, because when a unit
(b) square is removed, area decreases but perimeter increases.

For example,

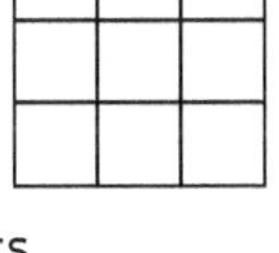

Area $= 9$ sq units
Perimeter $= 12$ units
When a square is removed.
Area $= 8$ sq units
Perimeter $= 14$ units

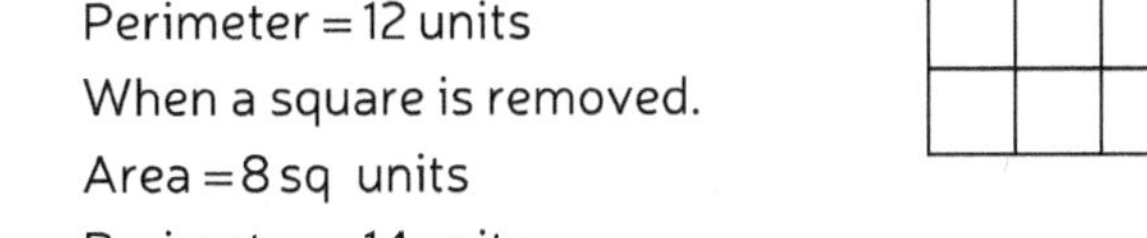

10. Given, breadth of the cut-out figure is 1/3rd the
(c) breadth of sheet.
$$\therefore \text{ Breadth of cut-out figure} = \frac{1}{3} \times 6 = 2\,m$$
and it can be seen from the diagram that length of the cut-out figure $= 12 \div 2 = 6\,m$
$\therefore$ Perimeter of cut-out figure
$$= 2 \times (\text{Length} + \text{Breadth})$$
$$= 2 \times (6 + 2) = 16\,m$$

11. The given track is in the shape of square.
(c) $\therefore$ Distance covered by biker
$$= 5 \times \text{Side of the track}$$
$$= 5 \times 30\,ft = 150\,ft$$

12. Here, boundary of garden A
(b)
$$= 2 \times (\text{Length} + \text{Breadth})$$
$$= 2 \times (12 + 8)\,m = 2 \times 20\,m = 40\,m$$
Boundary of garden $B = 2 \times (14 + 12)\,m$
$$= (2 \times 26)\,m = 52\,m$$

Boundary of garden $C = 2 \times (10 + 8)\,m$
$$= (2 \times 18)\,m = 36\,m$$
Boundary of garden $D = 2 \times (14 + 5)\,m$
$$= (2 \times 19)\,m = 38\,m$$
So, garden B has largest boundary.

13. From the above calculation, it is clear that
(c) garden C has smallest boundary.
If breadth of garden C is increased by 4 m, then perimeter $= 2 \times (10 + 12) = 44\,m$
Hence, Garden $D <$ Garden $A <$ Garden C
$$< \text{Garden } B$$
$\therefore$ Garden C is in the third position.

14. Area of the given figure
(d)
$$a = 12 \text{ sq units}$$
$$r = 7 \text{ sq units}$$
$$E = 10 \text{ sq units}$$
$$a = 12 \text{ sq units}$$
$$= (12 + 7 + 10 + 12) \text{ sq units} = 41 \text{ sq units}$$

15. Area is calculated by adding the total number of
(c) squares in a figure.
$$\therefore \text{ Area of Fig. } A \approx 9 \text{ sq units}$$
$$\text{Area of Fig. } B \approx 10 \text{ sq units}$$
$$\text{Area of Fig. } C \approx 20 \text{ sq units}$$
$$\text{Area of Fig. } D \approx 16 \text{ sq units}$$
So, C occupies the largest area.

16. From the above calculation, it is clear that Fig. B
(c) and Fig. C have a total area of approximately 30 sq units.

17. Radius of circle $= 3$ cm
(c) $\therefore$ Diameter of circle $= 2 \times 3$ cm $= 6$ cm
$\Rightarrow$ Side of square $=$ Diameter of circle $= 6$ cm
$\therefore$ Area of square $=$ Side $\times$ Side $= 6 \times 6 = 36\,cm^2$

18. Area of backyard $= 20$ sq ft
(a) Length of basketball court $= 5$ ft
Breadth of basketball court $= 4$ ft
$\therefore$ Area of basketball court
$$= (5 \times 4) \text{ sq ft} = 20 \text{ sq ft}$$
$\Rightarrow$ Area of backyard $=$ Area of basketball court

19. Perimeter $=$ Sum of lengths of all sides
(a)
$$= AB + BC + CD + DE + EF + FA$$
$$= [3.1 + 3.4 + 3.8 + 3.7 + (3.1 + 3.8)$$
$$+ (3.4 + 3.7)]\,cm = 28\,cm$$

20. Perimeter of shape I
(c)
$$= [50 + 60 + 15 + 80 + (50 + 15) + (80 - 60)]\,cm$$
$$= 290\,m$$

Perimeter of shape II
$$= [14 + 6 + 12 + 6 + (14 - 12) + (6 + 6)]\,cm = 52\,m$$

Perimeter of shape III
$$= [60 + 40 + 30 + 20 + (60 - 30) + (40 + 20)]\,m$$
$$= 240\,m$$

Perimeter of shape IV
$$= [22 + 21 + (29 - 22) + 26 + 29 + (26 - 21)]\,m$$
$$= 110\,m$$

Hence, option (c) is the correct answer.

21. Given, length of wall $= 28\,m$
(d)
and breadth of wall $= 21\,m$

$\therefore$ Area of wall $=$ Length $\times$ Breadth
$$= 28 \times 21 = 588\,m^2$$

Area of wall painted green $= \dfrac{1}{3} \times 588 = 196\,m^2$

Remaining area $= (588 - 196)\,m^2 = 392\,m^2$

So, area painted blue $= (392 \div 2)\,m^2 = 196\,m^2$

$\therefore$ Remaining area which is to be painted
$$= (392 - 196)\,m^2 = 196\,m^2$$

22. Perimeter of Fig. (i) $= (20 + 1 + 20 + 1)\,cm = 42\,cm$
(a)
Perimeter of Fig. (ii) $= (20 + 2 + 20 + 2)\,cm = 44\,cm$

$\therefore$ Required difference $= (44 - 42)\,cm = 2\,cm$

23. Length of park $= 65\,m$
(d)
Breadth of park $= 52\,m$

$\therefore$ Area of park $=$ Length $\times$ Breadth
$$= (65 \times 52)\,m^2 = 3380\,m^2$$

Area occupied by each girl
$$= 3380 \div 5 = 676\,m^2$$

$\therefore$ Area occupied by remaining 3 girls
$$= 676 \times 3 = 2028\,m^2$$

24. Perimeter of 1st square $= 40\,cm$
(b)
Perimeter of 2nd square $= 32\,cm$

Perimeter of 3rd square $=$ Perimeter of 1st square $-$ Perimeter of 2nd square
$$= (40 - 32)\,cm = 8\,cm$$

Since, perimeter of square $= 4 \times$ Side

$\Rightarrow$ Side of square $=$ Perimeter $\div 4$
$$= (8 \div 4)\,cm = 2\,cm$$

$\therefore$ Area of 3rd square $= (2 \times 2)\,cm = 4\,cm^2$

25. Here,
(b)
Length of horizontal strip $= 15\,cm$

Breadth of horizontal strip $= 5\,cm$

$\therefore$ Area of horizontal strip
$$= Length \times Breadth = 15 \times 5 = 75\,cm^2$$

Length of vertical strip $= 12\,cm$

Breadth of vertical strip $= 5\,cm$

$\therefore$ Area of vertical strip $= 12 \times 5 = 60\,cm^2$

$\Rightarrow$ Total area of strip $= (75 + 60)\,cm^2 = 135\,cm^2$

Now, area of flag $= (12 \times 15)\,cm^2 = 180\,cm^2$

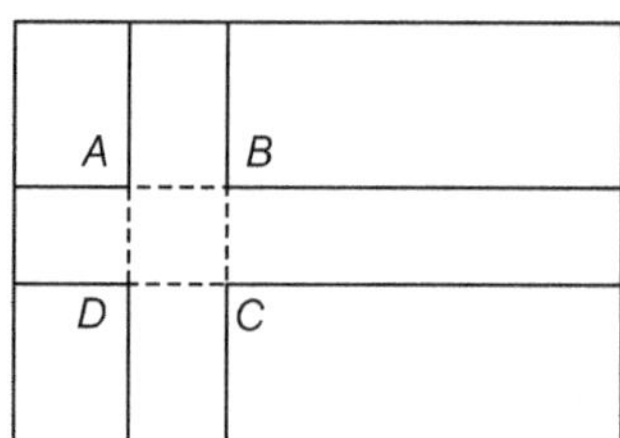

and area of square $ABCD =$ Side $\times$ Side
$$= 5 \times 5 = 25\,cm^2$$

$\therefore$ Required area $= (180 - 135) + 25$
$$= 45 + 25 = 70\,cm^2$$

10 Pattern

1. Here, in every step, number of squares is equal
(b) to the number of steps.

Hence, in 5th step, there will be 5 squares with the arrangement as in option (b).

2. Here, the letter E is taking $\dfrac{1}{4}$th turn in every step
(c)
in anti-clockwise direction.

So, next shape will be E.

3. From the given pattern, it is
(d) clear that next two shapes will be

4. Cyra is standing upright in every odd number of
(a) turns and is upside down in every even number
of turns, i.e. in Ist turn, Cyra is standing upright
and in IInd turn, Cyra is upside down and so on.

So, in 13th turn Cyra will be standing.

Mathematics Olympiad Class IV

5. Here, the first arrow is facing East and the next
(c) two arrows are facing West and so on.

So, in next two steps one arrow will be facing East and the next arrow will be facing West.

6. Here, the pattern is as follows:
(a) Number in Ist column × Number in IInd column = Number in IIIrd column.

i.e. In Ist row, $\quad 9 \times 4 = 36$

In IIIrd row, $\quad 12 \times 7 = 84$

∴ In IInd row, $\quad 5 \times A = 60$

$\Rightarrow \qquad \boxed{A = 12}$

7. Here, in each option except (b), the number of
(b) sides in outer shape is one more than the number of sides in inner shape.

8. Here, in every option except (d), letters in circles
(d) are vowels.

9. Here, in each option, except (d) the words have
(d) vowels and consonants but in option (d), the word consists of only consonants.

10. Here, in every option except (b), semi-circles
(b) are drawn, where the radius of no two semi-circles overlap but in option (b), radius overlaps and forms a complete circle.

11. Here, the figure must fit in the given pattern.
(d) Only, option (d) fits completely.

12. Here, each time 13 is added to get the next
(a) number.

i.e. $\qquad 39 + 13 = 52$

$52 + 13 = 65$

$65 + 13 = 78 = A$

$78 + 13 = 91$

$91 + 13 = 104 = B$

∴ $\qquad B - A = 104 - 78 = 26$

13. Here, the pattern is as follows :
(b) $\qquad 6 \times 4 = 24$

$3 \times 4 = 12$

$5 \times 4 = 20$

Similarly, $8 \times 4 = 32$

So, missing number is 32.

14.   I. a A b B c <u>C</u> d <u>D</u> a A b B
(c)   II. a b c a a b <u>c</u> a a b b c a a b <u>b</u> c <u>c</u>

  III. a b c d A b c d A B <u>c</u> d <u>A</u> B C <u>d</u>

  IV. a a B B c <u>c</u> A A <u>A</u> b b C <u>C</u>

15. Here, the previous terms are added to get the
(c) next term.

i.e. $\qquad 0 + 1 = 1$

$1 + 1 = 2$

$1 + 2 = 3$

and so on.

16. Here, in first figure, top circle is shaded, then in
(c) the following figure, triangle is shaded and in the next figure, bottom two circles are shaded and the pattern continues.

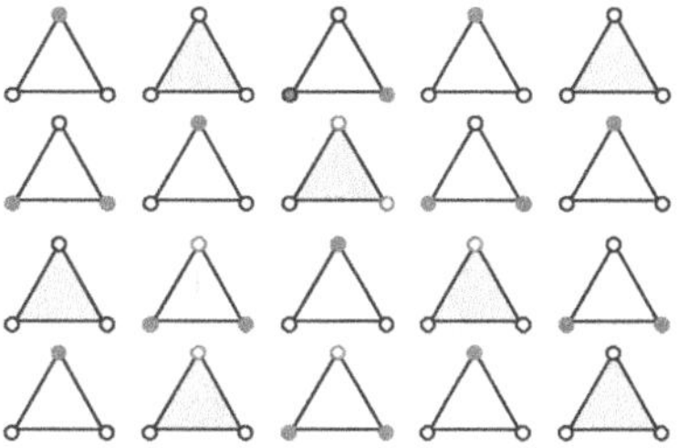

So, the number of figures leaving shaded triangles = 7

17.   I. Here, the numbers are consecutive prime
(d)   numbers.

Thus, next two numbers will be 11, 13.

  II. Here, the numbers are consecutive odd numbers.

So, next two numbers will be 9, 11.

  III. Here, first 2 is added and then 3 is added to get the next terms.

Therefore, next two numbers will be 13, 15.

  IV. Here, the numbers are obtained by adding 2, 4, 6, 8 and so on to the previous numbers.

Hence, next two numbers will be 22 and 32.

18. Here, the pattern is as follows :
(d) $\qquad 10000 - 800 = 9200$

$9200 - 800 = 8400$

$8400 - 800 = 7600$

So, none of the numbers is incorrect.

19. Here, 6 is subtracted from the numbers in the
(d) lower half to get the numbers in the upper half.

i.e. $\qquad 11 - 6 = 5$

$12 - 6 = 6$

Similarly, $25 - 6 = \boxed{19}$

Hence, option (d) is the correct answer.

20. Here, each letter is assigned a number
(c) according to its position in English alphabets.

A = 1, B = 2, C = 3, ..., X = 24, Y = 25, Z = 26

$$\therefore \quad E = 5, \ G = 7$$
$$K = 11, \ M = 13$$
$$P = 16, \ U = 21$$

Similarly, $\quad J = 10, \boxed{N = 14}$

21. I. True. Here, the pattern repeats itself after
(c) six steps and every step which is a multiple
of 6 is

and 54 is a multiple of 6.

II. False. Here, 7th shape from the last means
9th shape from the starting.

and 8th shape from the starting will be

III. True, if is removed, then 13th

shape will be

IV. False, the pattern with 27 steps will end
with

22. If 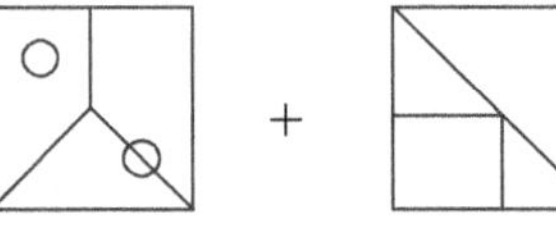
(c)

Then, the pattern will be A B C C B A A A.

23. Here, the dot inside circle is rotating in
(a) clockwise direction and the dot outside the
circle is rotating in anti-clockwise direction.

Hence, option (a) is the correct answer.

24. Here,
(c)

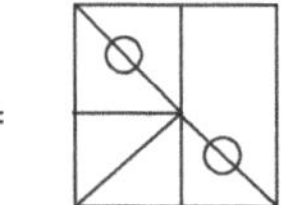

Hence, option (c) is the correct answer.

25. According to the question,
(a)

Days	Number of steps
1	2
2	4
3	6
4	8

$\therefore$ Number of steps is equal to the number of
days multiplied by 2.

i.e. $\quad 1 \times 2 = 2; \ 2 \times 2 = 4; \ 3 \times 2 = 6$

$\therefore \quad 17 \times 2 = 34$

11 Data Handling

1. Given the weights of 10 girls
(d) 28, 25, 20, 22, 19, 26, 30, 32, 22, 21.

Among these, 32 is the largest value.

So, the weight of heaviest girl is 32.

2. Rent = □□ = 1000 + 1000 = ₹ 2000
(b) Food = □□□□ = 1000 + 1000 + 1000 + 1000
$$= ₹ 4000$$

Transport = □ = ₹ 1000

Others = □□□ = 1000 + 1000 + 1000 = ₹ 3000

So, family spends the most on food.

3. The highest point scored is 10 by green team
(b) and hence 9 is the second highest points scored
by team blue.

4. Total number of children having their birthdays
(c) in July, August and September = 14

As per information,

No children have birthday in July and 4 children
have birthday in August.

$\therefore$ Number of children having their birthdays in
September = 14 − 4 = 10

5. Total sale of books

(c)

$$= 200 + 150 + 300 + 250$$
$$= 900$$

6. Since, Anne > Jenny > Karen > Jai

(c)

$\Rightarrow$ Anne is the tallest child.

$\therefore \qquad B = $ Anne

The second tallest child is Jenny.

$\therefore \qquad C = $ Jenny

The third tallest child is Karen.

$\therefore \qquad D = $ Karen

and the smallest child is Jai.

$\therefore \qquad A = $ Jai

7. From the given pie chart, it is clear that

(b) Half of the customers like fries.

One-fourth of the customers like burger.

One-fourth of the customers like cold coffee.

Hence, option (b) is true.

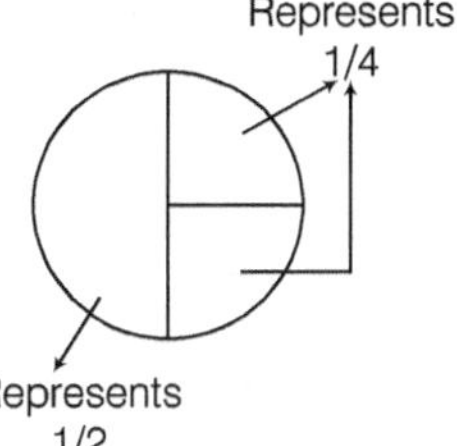

8. I. True (by definition)

(b) II. True (by definition)

III. True

IV. False. In the bar graph, the data is represented using bars.

9. From a total of 28 children, 14 are acting which

(c) is half of 25 ($28 \div 2 = 14$).

7 are collecting dresses, which is one-fourth of 28 ($28 \div 4 = 7$).

and again 7 are making sets which is one-fourth of 28 ($28 \div 4 = 7$).

$\therefore$ Appropriate pie chart will be

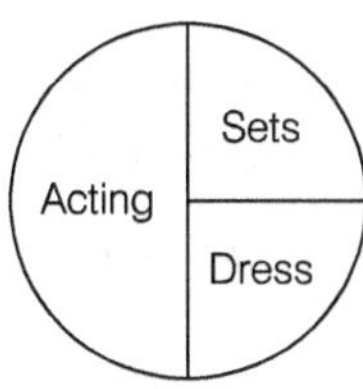

10. Since, marks of Krista is neither increasing

(c) constantly nor decreasing.

So, the performance of Krista cannot be determined.

11. From the given graph, it is clear that

(d) Five days, Anne practiced for $\dfrac{1}{4}$ hour.

Three days, Anna practiced for $\dfrac{3}{4}$ hour.

Two days, Anna practiced for $1\dfrac{1}{2}$ hours.

One day, Anna practiced for $1\dfrac{3}{4}$ hours.

$\therefore$ Total time that Anna practiced piano over the 11 days

$$= 5 \times \frac{1}{4} + 3 \times \frac{3}{4} + 2 \times 1\frac{1}{2} + 1\frac{3}{4}$$

$$= \frac{5}{4} + \frac{9}{4} + 2 \times \frac{3}{2} + \frac{7}{4} = \frac{5}{4} + \frac{9}{4} + 3 + \frac{7}{4}$$

$$= \frac{5 + 9 + 12 + 7}{4} = \frac{33}{4} = 8\frac{1}{4}$$

12.

(c)

Day	Number of ice-creams
1st	20
2nd	16
3rd	14
4th	18

From the above data, it is clear that on 3rd day, 14 ice-creams were sold.

13. From the data (in Q. No. 12), it is clear that on

(d) days 1 and 2, total of 36 ice-creams were sold.

14.

(d)

Day	Number of cars
A–Monday	10
B–Tuesday	12
C–Wednesday	4
D–Thursday	5
E–Friday	7

From the above data, it is clear that the order is $4 < 5 < 7 < 10 < 12$, i.e. $C < D < E < A < B$.

15. As per given data,

(d) Maths Olympiad = 12

Science Olympiad = 8

English Olympiad = 6

Computer Olympiad = 14

It is clear that most of the students are interested in Computer Olympiad, i.e. 14.

16. Number of children interested in Maths

(c) Olympiad = 12

Number of children interested in English Olympiad = 6

$\therefore$ Required difference = $12 - 6 = 6$

17. Total number of houses $= 30$
(c) Total number of houses with dog, cat, tortoise and parrot as their pet

$$= 12 + 7 + 1 + 5 = 25$$

$\therefore$ Number of houses with rabbit as their pet

$$= 30 - 25 = 5$$

18. The given bar graph show marks obtained by a
(d) student in four subjects in the session of 2014-15.

Hence, option (d) is correct.

19. The student scored second highest marks in
(d) Science, i.e. 50.

Since, marks in English $= 40$

$$\text{marks in Hindi} = 30$$
$$\text{marks in Maths} = 60$$
$$\text{marks in Science} = 50$$

20. Marks scored in English $= 40$
(b) and $\dfrac{3}{4}$ of $40 = 30 =$ Marks scored in Hindi

Hence, in Hindi marks is $\dfrac{3}{4}$ of marks in English.

21. From the graph, it is clear that $\dfrac{1}{4}$ of the campers
(d) choose canoeing as their favourite activity.

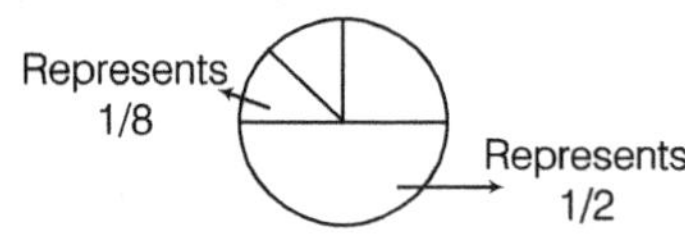

22. Fraction of children who choose crafts $= \dfrac{1}{8}$
(a)

Fraction of children who choose horse riding $= \dfrac{1}{2}$

$\therefore$ Total fraction $= \dfrac{1}{8} + \dfrac{1}{2} = \dfrac{1+4}{8} = \dfrac{5}{8}$

Practice Set 1

1. Given, population of city $= 145526$
(d) Since, $\qquad 5526 > 5000$

$\therefore 145526$ when rounded off to nearest thousand will become 146000.

2. From the given numbers, when 18 is multiplied
(c) by 19, the product is 342.

i.e. $\qquad 18 \times 19 = 342$

3. We have,
(c)

(a) $\dfrac{1 \times 4}{6 \times 4} = \dfrac{4}{24}$

(b) $\dfrac{1 \times 3}{8 \times 3} = \dfrac{3}{24}$

(c) $\dfrac{2 \times 6}{4 \times 6} = \dfrac{12}{24}$

(d) $\dfrac{24}{24}$

Since, it is given that Tancy studied for more number of hours on Tuesday than on Monday.

Among the given options, only (c) represents hours more than 6.

$\therefore$ Tancy studied for 12 hours on Tuesday out of 24 hours.

4. $\dfrac{3}{4} < \dfrac{9}{10}$ because $\dfrac{3}{4}$ is less than $\dfrac{4}{5}$ and $\dfrac{9}{10}$ is greater
(d) than $\dfrac{4}{5}$.

5. Since, $0.42 = \dfrac{42}{100}$
(b)

So, Mia read 42 pages out of 100.

6. Since, $4.5\,\text{kg} = 4500\,\text{g}$ and $4500\,\text{g} \div 300\,\text{g} = 15$
(c) $\therefore$ Fifteen 300 g of sugar packets are required to make 4.5 kg.

7. Angle is formed by two rays or two line
(b) segments with a common end point.

8. From the figure it is clear that, the container has
(b) $2\dfrac{1}{5}$ cup of juice.

9. Here, Area of rectangle $A =$ Length $\times$ Breadth
(c) $$= 8.5 \times 2 = 17 \text{ sq cm}$$

Perimeter of rectangle A

$$= 2 \times (\text{Length} + \text{Breadth})$$
$$= 2 \times (8.5 + 2)$$
$$= 2 \times 10.5 = 21 \text{ cm}$$

Mathematics Olympiad Class IV

Similarly,

Area of rectangle $B = 20$ cm

Perimeter of rectangle $B = 18$ cm

and since square is also a rectangle.

$\therefore$ Area of rectangle $C = 16$ cm

and perimeter of rectangle $C = 16$ cm

$\therefore$ Perimeter of rectangle $A >$ Area of rectangle A

and

Perimeter of rectangle $C =$ Area of rectangle C

10. Since, George wants to distribute 30 pencils and
(c) 20 pens among maximum number of children.

$\therefore$ Will find the HCF of 30 and 20.

$$30 = 2 \times 3 \times 5$$
$$20 = 2 \times 2 \times 5$$

$\therefore$ HCF (30, 20) $= 10$

So, 30 pencils and 20 pens can be divided equally among 10 children.

Thus, each child will have 3 pencils (30 $\div$ 10) and 2 pens (20 $\div$ 10).

Cost of 3 pencils $= 5 \times 3 = ₹ 15$

Cost of 2 pens $= 2 \times 10 = ₹ 20$

Hence, a child owe (₹ 20 + ₹ 15) $= ₹ 35$ to Greoge.

11. The letters that cannot be folded into halves are
(a) F, G, J, L, N, P, Q, R, S, Z, i.e. 10.

12.
(b)

Toppings	Number of votes
Cheese	3
Pepperoni	6
Sausage	4
Mushroom	0
Onion	2

From the above data, it is clear that Sausage is the group's second favourite type of pizza.

13. Total money in piggy bank I $= ₹ 34.5$
(a) Total money in piggy bank II $= ₹ 80$

$\therefore$ Total money in both piggy banks

$$= ₹ 80 + ₹ 34.5 = ₹ 114.5$$

Since, $\qquad 4 < 5$

So, total money in both piggy banks rounded off to nearest ten is ₹ 110.

14. From the graph, it is clear that there were 160
(c) spectators at the boxing event.

15. Maximum number of spectators are in
(d) swimming $= 200$

Minimum number of spectators are in weight lifting $= 80$

So, required difference $= 200 - 80 = 120$

Practice Set ❷

1. Number of pieces of candy which could be in
(c) Louisa's bag $=$ LCM (2, 3, 5) $= 30$

2. Number of scoops required by each child $= 2$
(c)
Total number of children $= 18$

Number of scoops in one container $= 6$

Since, $\qquad 6 \div 2 = 3$

$\Rightarrow$ Each container can serve 3 children.

$\therefore$ Number of containers required $= 18 \div 3 = 6$

Alternate Method

The total number of scoops of ice-creams required for 18 children

$$= 2 \times 18 = 36$$

Since, 6 scoopes of ice-cream in 1 container.

So, required container $= \dfrac{36}{6} = 6$

3. The maximum number which Anouk can get on
(d) his both dice is 6.

As, $\qquad 6 + 6 = 12$

So, Anouk can move a maximum of 12 squares by throwing both the dice once.

4. From the clues, we have that multiples of 5
(b) which are less than 27 are 5, 10, 15, 20, 25. But the number should be even. So, we have the choice between 10 and 20.

Also, the number should be a factor of 10.

So, 10 is the required number.

5. Here, we have the following number of obtuse
(c) angles from each figure

(a) Number of obtuse angles $= 3$

(b) Number of obtuse angles $= 0$

(c) Number of obtuse angles $=8$

(d) Number of obtuse angles $=6$

$\therefore$ Hence, option (c) has maximum number of obtuse angles.

6. If the HCF of first two multiples of a number is
(b) one of the numbers, then their LCM is the other number.

For example, HCF of first two multiples of 6, i.e. 6 and 12 is 6 and their LCM is 12.

7. Length of the chart paper $=13\,cm$
(b)
Breadth of the chart paper $=8\,cm$

$\therefore$ Area of the chart paper $=$ Length $\times$ Breadth
$$= 13 \times 8$$
$$= 104\,cm^2$$

Area occupied by each stamp $= 2\,cm^2$

$\therefore$ Number of stamps that could be placed in the chart paper $= 104 \div 2 = 52$

8.
(d)

1.25	3.98	4.84	6.53
$+\ 2.95$	$\times\ 4$	$\div\ 2$	$-\ 1.64$
4.2	15.92	2.42	4.89

Arranging in decreasing order, we get

$$15.92 < 4.89 < 4.2 < 2.42$$
$$\text{T} \qquad \text{A} \qquad \text{M} \qquad \text{E}$$

9. Given, $(8 \times 2) \times 5 = 16 \times 5 = 80$
(c)
From option (c), $8 \times (2 \times 5) = 8 \times 10 = 80$

10. Given,
(a)
Number of words in first line $= 7$

Number of words in second line $= 12$

Number of words in third line $= 17$

and so on.

$\therefore$ The pattern is

$$2\text{nd line} \rightarrow 7 + 5 = 12$$
$$3\text{rd line} \rightarrow 12 + 5 = 17$$
$$4\text{th line} \rightarrow 17 + 5 = 22$$
$$5\text{th line} \rightarrow 22 + 5 = 27$$
$$6\text{th line} \rightarrow 27 + 5 = 32$$
$$7\text{th line} \rightarrow 32 + 5 = 37$$
$$8\text{th line} \rightarrow 37 + 5 = 42$$

So, there will be 42 words in the eighth line.

11. Number of classes from 15th April till 19th June
(c) excluding Sunday
$$= (16 + 31 + 19) - 9 = 66 - 9 = 57$$

Fees of one hour $= ₹\,150$

$\therefore$ Total fees $= ₹\,150 \times 57$
$$= ₹\,8550$$

12. Here, the numbers on the corners add upto 17
(c) and the numbers in the middle also add upto 17.

i.e. $\qquad 4 + 7 + 3 + 3 = 17$

and $\qquad 3 + 6 + ? + 5 = 17$

$\Rightarrow \qquad\qquad 14 + ? = 17$

$\Rightarrow \qquad\qquad ? = 17 - 14 = 3$

13. Figure (a) shows the correct number of stairs
(a) Eeva has climbed.

Because $\dfrac{15}{25} = \dfrac{3 \times 5}{5 \times 5}$

Hence, $\dfrac{15}{25}$ is equivalent to $\dfrac{3}{5}$.

14.
(d)

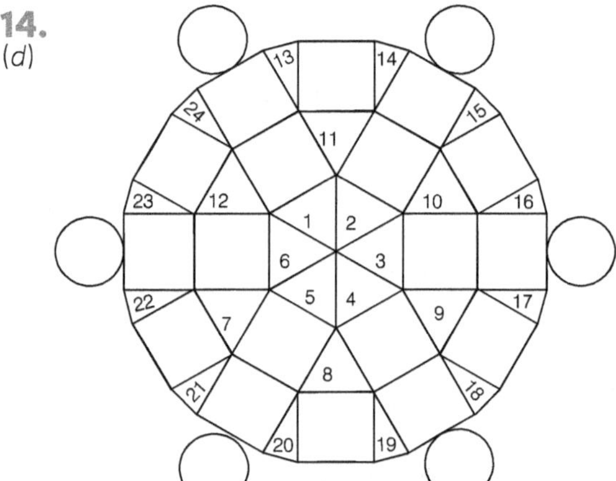

From the figure, it is clear that there are 24 triangles in the given figure.

15. Time at which Krista and her friends started
(b) planting $= 5:00\,pm$

Time required to plant one sapling $= 30\,minutes$

Number of plants planted on Tuesday $= 6$

$\therefore$ Time required to plant 6 saplings
$$= 6 \times 30 = 180\,minutes = 3\,hours$$

So, Krista and her friends get their work done at $(5 + 3) = 8:00\,pm$.